Anne Scott-James was born in 1913 and educated at St Paul's Girls' School and Somerville College, Oxford. In 1934 she joined the Editorial Staff of *Vogue* and for over thirty years has worked on newspapers and periodicals: as Woman's Editor on *Picture Post* (1941–5); Editor of *Harper's Bazaar* (1945–51); Woman's Editor on the *Sunday Express* (1953–7); Woman's Adviser to Beaverbrook Newspapers (1959–60), and Columnist on the *Daily Mail* (1960–8). Since 1968 she has been a freelance journalist and broadcaster on radio and television. She was a Member of the Council of the Royal Council of Art in 1948–51 and again in 1954–6, is a Member of Council of the Royal Horticultural Society and is the author of *In the Mink* (1952), *Down to Earth* (1971) and *Sissinghurst: The Making of a Garden* (1975).

Osbert Lancaster was born in 1908 and educated at Charterhouse and Lincoln College, Oxford. In 1939 he joined the *Daily Express* as a cartoonist, and between 1940 and 1947 he worked in the News Department of the Foreign Office, was attached to H.M. Embassy in Athens and was Sydney Jones Lecturer in Art at Liverpool University. Since 1969 he has been Adviser to the G.L.C. Historic Buildings Board and is Governor of King Edward School, King's Lynn. An Hon. D.Lit. of the Universities of Birmingham, Newcastle upon Tyne, St Andrews and Oxford, he is a Fellow of University College, London, an Honorary Fellow of the Royal Institute of British Architects, was awarded the C.B.E. in 1953 and knighted in 1975.

He has designed theatre décors for productions at Sadler's Wells, Covent Garden and Glyndebourne. His publications include *Pillar to Post*, *Classical Landscape with Figures*, *The Saracen's Head*, *Façades and Faces*, *A Cartoon History of Architecture*, two volumes of autobiography (*All Done From Memory* and *With an Eye to the Future*) and *The Littlehampton Bequest*.

ANNE SCOTT-JAMES

OSBERT LANCASTER

The Pleasure Garden

An Illustrated History of
British Gardening

Penguin Books

Penguin Books Ltd, Harmondsworth, Middlesex, England
Penguin Books, 625 Madison Avenue, New York 10022, U.S.A.
Penguin Books Australia Ltd, Ringwood, Victoria, Australia
Penguin Books Canada Ltd, 2801 John Street, Markham, Ontario, Canada L3R 1BA
Penguin Books (N.Z.) Ltd, 182–190 Wairau Road, Auckland 10, New Zealand

First published by John Murray 1977
Published in Penguin Books 1979

Made and printed in Great Britain by
Butler & Tanner Ltd, Frome and London

For Jock and Diana

CONTENTS

ACKNOWLEDGEMENTS

SCARCELY A CHAPTER of this book could have been written without the help of Mr Peter Stageman, Librarian of the incomparable Royal Horticultural Society Lindley Library. I am also indebted for botanical research and for proof-reading to Miss Sandra Raphael and for research on the later chapters to Miss Cara Lancaster. Professor Barry Cunliffe, the archaeologist of Fishbourne, was kind enough to check my chapter on the Romano-British garden; Mr George Clarke of Stowe School guided me round the Stowe landscape and gave me much help with the chapter on the Landscape; and Mr Ashley Barker of the Greater London Council sorted out some of my difficulties over the history of London squares. At Hestercombe I gladly acknowledge the help and hospitality of the Chief Fire Officer of the Somerset County Fire Brigade and of Miss Lorna McRobie of the Somerset County Architect's Landscape Section. Of the many owners of historic gardens who have given me time and help I must particularly thank Mrs Robin Bagot of Levens Hall, Cumbria, and Mrs David Verey of Barnsley House, Gloucestershire.

APOLOGIA

THIS IS NOT a book by me illustrated by Osbert Lancaster. Where a book exists of the breadth and scholarship of Miles Hadfield's *History of British Gardening*, it would be folly to attempt to tread the same ground. I have merely written a series of essays to accompany a set of drawings on which my husband was suddenly and unexpectedly moved to embark.

This marital partnership has not been wholly easy. Each of us has been accustomed to plough a lone furrow, and in double harness we often pulled in different ways. While I was sweating over Pliny, he tended to be musing on his youth in a London square. When I was studying Canon Raven on the mediaeval naturalists, he would demand a list of plants suitable for the Dutch garden to be delivered in ten minutes, and then most of my suggestions would prove unsuitable for illustration. Sometimes the only plant he felt like drawing was a yucca, with its strong architectural outlines, and I am surprised that there is not a yucca in every sketch, from the Romano-British period onward.

Some of the terms I have used in the book are open to pedantic criticism, but I have used them in their generally accepted meaning. It is true that 'formal' could mean anything with a form, including a wild and erratic form, but you know and I know, without further explanation, that in gardening 'formal' means 'geometric'.

I have said several times in the text, but would like to stress at the start, that though this book shows a progression of garden styles, the changes were never abrupt. Each style has its seeds in the past, its flowers in the present, and its fruits in the future.

Anne Scott-James

1

ROMAN BRITAIN

THE ROMANS, among their other achievements, invented the British country gentleman. The Celts they conquered were countrymen by nature, and the Romans added the polish. Tacitus, shrewdest and wryest of historians, says that his father-in-law, Agricola, governor of Britain for seven years in the reigns of Vespasian and Domitian, taught the natives the Roman way of life, introducing them to luxurious buildings and elegant clothes, to heated baths and convivial dinner parties. He adds, somewhat patronizingly, that the British were proud of their new culture, though their Romanization was merely a tool of imperial policy.

With the general lift in the style of living—with the fine buildings and good cooking, the Latin conversation and the fashionable clothes (it soon became smart to wear a toga)—came the Roman art of gardening. It has always seemed fair to assume that a stylish villa in Britain had a garden very like an Italian garden, but with a more enclosed layout to suit the climate and without the tender plants, like olives and myrtles. Experienced colonists carry their style of living around when they travel, and just as the English mem-sahib tried to grow herbaceous borders in India and the Dutch made canals in Batavia (disastrously, because they stank), so the Romans would surely have imported the Italian garden here.

Today, the guesswork can be taken as fact. In 1961, the excavation began of a large Romano-British villa at Fishbourne, on the Sussex coast, and for the first time the archaeologists fully explored the garden as well as the buildings. The garden they reconstructed was so like an Italian garden of the period in design, cultivation and setting that one must digress to see what the Italian original was like.

The Italian garden we know most about is that of the Younger Pliny's

Tuscan villa, which he described in a long and not wholly lucid letter written in about A.D. 100—slightly later than Fishbourne, but this is immaterial, for the style was crystallizing as early as the reign of Augustus. Pliny's garden was completely formal, shaped like a horse-shoe, and was cut by symmetrical rows of trees and hedges into cool, shady avenues for walking and talking, Pliny doubtless hogging the conversation. Many of the plants were pleached or trained. Vines and roses were trained to pergolas; fruit-trees were trained espalier-fashion; rows of trees were linked by festoons of trained ivy and evergreens were clipped with military precision. Topiary had come in at about the time of Augustus and the Romans were enchanted with it. Pliny's hedges were clipped into fantastic shapes, such as animals or letters of the alphabet, and Pliny's name was cut out in box, as was the name of his gardener, an early example of the friendship which great men and their gardeners have often shared—one thinks of the 6th Duke of Devonshire and Joseph Paxton. Pliny was not what we think of as a plantsman, but seems to have regarded plants as a material like brick or marble. Shade and foliage he appreciated, but the individual plant had little message for him, though he liked scented plants and had a violet bed at his winter villa by the sea.

Outside the formal garden was a semi-wild garden (a flash forward to the English 'wilderness' of Tudor times and after) linking it with the landscape, with loosely planted groves and meandering walks beside a natural stream. There were also a vegetable garden and an apiary tucked out of sight. Throughout the whole estate there was a mass of ornamentation. It was positively littered with porticoes, pavilions, obelisks, fountains, seats, bathing and picnic places, columns and trellises.

But if it was over-furnished and too artificial for our taste, a Roman garden had two great merits. It was designed to give fine views of the surrounding country and, if Pliny was insensitive to garden plants, he was eloquent about the Italian landscape. And the garden was cultivated to a high standard. Pliny's uncle, author of the *Natural History*, is the authority here and, though his botany is weak, his gardening knowledge is highly sophisticated. Most of his tips on planting, manuring, irrigating, pruning, forcing and so on hold good today. Again, it is clear that with

the exception of roses, lilies, violets and other plants chosen for their scent, plants were grown for utility rather than beauty. The Romans grew plants to eat and to flavour food, to make wine and chaplets, for dyes and aphrodisiacs, beauty preparations and perfumes, and to cure every known ailment from boils to asthma, from menopausal pains to snakebite, but they did not *love* flowers. The modern gardener is shocked by their treatment of roses, of which thousands were torn to pieces to make petal mattresses for banquets, necessary, perhaps, to deaden the unsavoury smells.

The Roman town garden, like the country garden, was theatrical and crowded with ornament, as we see in the well-preserved paintings of Pompeii. A garden in the peristyle (or courtyard) of a town house was furnished with fountains, statues, columns, vases and other status symbols, and painted walls, frescoed with *trompe-l'œil* trees and flowers, gave an illusion of size.

The formal, extravagant style of pleasure garden came to Britain from Italy in the 1st century. One hopes that the native landowner tempered its excesses with a little Celtic good taste, but more likely he was besotted by all the foreign novelties, and one suspects that the owner of Fishbourne in its prime—probably a tribal king called Cogidubnus in about A.D. 75 —had his name cut out in box.

The similarity of Fishbourne to Italian villas is remarkable; evidence of planting trenches, post-holes, soil enrichment and decorative stonework shows that it was wholly Roman in design and decoration. The villa, which was possibly a palace, a splendid affair with handsome porticoes and colonnades, was built round a large peristyle or arcaded courtyard, planted as a formal garden. The courtyard was bisected by a wide central path, flanked by hedges two or three tiers deep, almost certainly of box, clipped into alcoves for statues or seats. There were narrower, hedge-lined paths for peripatetics, trained fruit-trees, probably rose-beds, and piped water bubbling up in decorative basins of Purbeck marble. Most exciting discovery of all, one external wall of the villa was frescoed with foliage and roses, a toy landscape exactly like those on the garden walls of houses at Pompeii.

Outside the villa, on the seaward side, was a terrace informally planted to link house with landscape, as in Pliny's villas. From this terrace the owner had a spectacular view of the coast and the shipping, and he must have enjoyed reclining on a seat and admiring the scenery, like Pliny at his seaside villa, but more warmly wrapped up.

Discreetly placed out of sight there was a vegetable garden, manured with kitchen refuse.

The plants can only be guessed at, but roses, box and other evergreens are a near-certainty, and there were probably lilies, acanthus, rosemary, ivy, native wild flowers like violets and periwinkles, and a good range of herbs and hardy vegetables such as cabbage, leeks, onions, garlic, cucumber and broad beans. The orchard would include apples, pears and cherries. Vines probably came to Britain later, in the 3rd century, having been banned until then by imperial decree to protect the Italian wine trade.

Fishbourne is an exceptionally fine Roman villa, but by no means the largest in Britain. Woodchester and other aristocratic villas would have had both formal and landscape gardens comparable in scale. Smaller villas would have had a combined pleasure and vegetable garden inside a courtyard. The meanest villas would have had utility gardens only. All the important gardens were in the open country, an amenity of the villa-estates which belonged to the native, but Romanized, British upper classes. Most of the British lived in the country throughout the Roman occupation, while Roman-born officials, traders and retired legionaries lived in the towns, which were small but rich in architecture. The plans of Silchester show quite spacious gardens and presumably in denser towns there were roof, terrace, patio and pot gardens as in Rome itself.

The villas were widely, but not evenly distributed throughout Britain, for under Roman rule, country society split, rich and poor settling in different areas. The upper classes chose upland districts, like the Cotswolds, with a light, well-drained soil, the easiest soil to work without mechanical tools. An acid soil had not yet become the gardener's favourite medium, and when a villa was built on acid soil, as at Fishbourne, which is clay over gravel, the soil was marled.

The Celts had always been good farmers, and landscaping a garden was a natural occupation for a British country gentleman who had picked up some Roman culture. There must have been thousands who, enjoying all sorts of other Roman artistic delights, such as mosaic pavements, wall-paintings and pottery, also gardened in the Roman manner throughout the four centuries of the prosperity of the villa-estates. It was not until after A.D. 400 that the system fell apart.

2

THE MONASTIC GARDEN

AFTER THE RETREAT of the legions, English garden history vanished into the maw of the Dark Ages, not to reappear until after the Norman conquest. The known facts about Anglo-Saxon gardening are mere crumbs—herbs, fruits and vegetables were grown and there were many vineyards in the south.

Early mediaeval records from the 12th century onwards are more substantial, though open to various interpretations. How far was Chaucer, writing lyrically of flowery meads, a reporter of the English scene and how far was he a widely travelled poet who drew on his knowledge of France and Italy? How can one reconcile the almost total absence of realistic flower painting and sculpture in mediaeval England with the rare exception, like the 13th-century leaf carvings at Southwell, in Nottinghamshire, which show the most sensitive observation? Such problems may never be finally resolved.

The most solid fact to emerge is that the important gardeners were the monks (also the nuns, who are not always given their share of the credit). The monks had the brains, knowledge and organization to make good gardens. They had the impetus, since a monastery had to be self-supporting. Their lives were relatively secure and they could choose rich valley land to live on while the barons were building their castles on defensible but infertile hilltops. They were in close touch with monasteries on the Continent, so that when lost Roman skills returned to Europe, English monks would acquire them too. And, often, a monastery was doctor's surgery and apothecary's shop to a whole neighbourhood, so that the monastic garden was of public importance, though doubtless the peasants did a lot of self-doctoring and gathered their simples wild.

The earliest pictorial record of an English monastic garden is a charming

15

sketch-plan of the priory of Christ Church, Canterbury, which scholars date as 1165. It shows a cloistered courtyard (descendant of the Roman peristyle) with a small herb garden inside near the infirmary, and an orchard, vineyard and fishponds outside. One of the foremost historians of the mediaeval garden, Alicia Amherst, believed that the pattern of monastery gardens changed little from early Norman times until the Reformation. There would always be a garden inside the cloisters for walking and contemplation, usually grassed and with a central well or fountain; a herb-and-vegetable plot somewhere inside the walls; usually a separate physic garden next to the infirmary; and, in the case of a large monastery, separate private gardens for the senior monks.

The vegetable plots were surprisingly small, divided into neat oblong beds for different crops. Garlic, shallots, parsley, chervil, lettuce, savory, hyssop, fennel, cabbage, corncockle, onions, leeks, celery, coriander, dill, poppy, radishes, carrots and beets appear in very early records. Cultivation was intense and the layout skilful. William Cobbett, in *The English Gardener* (1829), says that he never saw a kitchen garden so beautifully organized for sunshine, shelter and moisture as that at Waverley Abbey, a Cistercian foundation which he had seen in his youth almost unaltered from its original plan. The kitchen garden was sited under the shelter of a hill and had a thick wall on the north side; below the wall was a strip of sloping land, facing south, for early vegetables, then a flat terrace for the main crops, all watered by the River Wey. Seeing the site again fifty years later, Cobbett reported that a rich new proprietor had wrecked the ancient layout and made a larger, less productive garden at the top of the hill.

As well as kitchen and physic gardens, most monasteries had land outside the walls for orchards, vineyards, fishponds, beanfields, perhaps osier beds, woodland and farmland, making up, in the case of a rich monastery, a very large estate. A good range of fruit was grown in choice as well as common varieties (for monks were not free from greed), most of the best kinds being French—apples, pears, cherries, quinces, mulberries, medlars, grapes, peaches, strawberries, nuts and probably figs—but the vegetables of the refectory must have been as monotonous as those at

a public school. Beans, beans, beans *ad nauseam* (there were broad beans only), with peas, onions and leeks, occur in most surviving account books.

The monks would hope to have a surplus of produce to sell, but crops could fail for the man of God as well as for the laity, and sometimes the books failed to balance, or the monastery had to buy in seeds.

What about flowers? We know pretty well what flowers were grown in the Middle Ages—roses and lilies were the favourites, then irises, violets, hollyhocks, honeysuckle, peonies, lavender, periwinkles and columbines, and there were dozens of unimproved wild flowers for herbal use. It is the mediaeval attitude to flowers which is hard to penetrate. Some scholars hold that the mediaeval world viewed the whole of nature in mystic terms, that a lily was admired as an emblem of purity, a daisy as a symbol of humility, and a rose taught the lesson that pleasure is entangled with thorns. In other words, flowers had more symbolic than aesthetic appeal. Certainly the whole of mediaeval life in England was dominated by the Church, and a scientific interest in nature was as yet unborn.

However that may be, a few flowers were grown in monasteries for church decoration and for chaplets, which were worn by priests for ceremonies, as in pagan times, until the Reformation. And two small episodes relating to the abbey of Romsey indicate a love of flowers for sheer beauty. In 1093, William Rufus, bent on meeting a young lady who was living there in the care of the abbess, entered the cloister with the frail excuse of inspecting the roses; and at some time in the 12th or 13th century, a rose with stalk and leaves was sealed into the abbey wall for some romantic or religious reason, to be found there by workmen in 1976. Clearly the rose garden of this nunnery was something of a beauty spot, an early sign, perhaps, of the flower garden as a woman's province.

The first useful list of mediaeval flowers comes to us from Alexander Neckham, an abbot of Cirencester in the 12th century. His treatise, *De Naturis Rerum*, is myth-ridden and quaint and derivative from early Latin authors, but it is better than nothing. He says the garden is to be adorned with roses, lilies, heliotrope, violets, mandrake, daffodils and acanthus, in addition to vegetables and culinary and physic herbs. Many of these, such as borage, poppies, cornflowers, foxgloves, gentians, would of course be decorative as well as useful, but for the most part the monastery garden was subdued in colour, and the flowers were small.

3

THE PLEASAUNCE

THE MONKS were the most learned gardeners in the Middle Ages, but there were secular gardens too. Everyone with a plot, however small, grew herbs, and there were thriving vegetable market gardens in and just outside the towns, particularly London, which in the 12th century was a garden city. But palaces, castles, town houses and manor houses also had pleasure gardens.

These were small and quite naïve. A plot enclosed by a wall, hedge, railing or wattle fence, with a few square beds, some trees, an arbour and a turfed seat, a bit of trellis with roses and a group of lilies was held to make up a delectable garden. The arbour, of trellis or trained trees intertwined with roses, honeysuckle or a plant which in some mediaeval pictures looks suspiciously like the greater bindweed, was an essential feature. This little garden might lead into an orchard or flowery mead, where girls sat on the grass and wove garlands while their young men dallied and sometimes advanced a loving hand to stroke an amenable breast or thigh. Garland-weaving seems to have taken the place now held by knitting as a useful way of passing the time and garlands were worn by all and sundry—even Chaucer's appalling Summoner sported a garland, an incongruous finish to his fat and spotty face.

A grander garden, especially as we enter the Tudor period, might have more imposing features, such as a chunky fountain, a maze or a mount— an artificial hillock with a spiral path to the top which started life as a lookout place inside the boundary walls of castle or palace, and developed into a rather irrelevant garden decoration.

Except for lilies and roses, both single and double, the flowers were mostly those of ditch and field, and nobody looked for more. Chaucer is said to have loved gardens, and Emilie's garden in the Knight's Tale, where Palamon and Arcite watched her walking from their prison

window, is a celebrated example; but when you come down to brass tacks, his flower knowledge was lamentable. Emilie 'Gathereth flowers party white and red, To make a subtle garland for her head' does not reveal deep botanical interest. He was equally vague in his translation of *The Romance of the Rose*:

> And flowers yellow, white and red,
> Such plenty grew there never in mead.
> Full gay was all the ground, and quaint
> And powdered as men had it paint.

What Chaucer really loved was nature, green meadows sprinkled with daisies, the freshness of the month of May, streams and sunshine, raindrops hanging in the leaves, and the song of 'the busy lark'. He was rather better on trees than on flowers, listing twenty kinds which were used to make unlucky Arcite's funeral pyre.

Soon after Chaucer's death in 1400, James I of Scotland was imprisoned at Windsor Castle and wrote a wistful poem about the lovely garden he could see from his window. This real garden was very like Emilie's imaginary garden, with not much more than leafy arbours, shady alleys, juniper trees, hawthorn hedges and a nightingale.

The conclusion must be that mediaeval gardens were loved, but that they were elementary. The gardeners were skilled in propagating roses and fruit trees, in pruning, and in the training of good hedges, but most of the plants grown were unimproved wild plants. In 1440, or possibly earlier, the first known how-to-do-it gardening book in the English language was written, *The Feate of Gardening*, by Jon Gardener, presumably a *nom-de-plume* like 'Mr Blossom'. The author tells his readers how to grow some hundred different plants, mostly wild herbs, plus a few uninteresting vegetables, and the text, though sensible, is uninspired. Only a single manuscript copy survives today, but the fact that this little treatise was written in English shows that there was a secular public beginning to prick up its ears for gardening advice.

The semi-darkness of the whole mediaeval period in garden history is further confused by the various disasters which afflicted the nation. The

Black Death, cutting the population by a third or even a half, must have all but destroyed the arts and crafts, and when they were nicely recovering, they received another blow from the Wars of the Roses. For several centuries gardening lurched forwards and back again, and made no steady progress until the Tudors were well into their stride.

4

TUDOR AND JACOBEAN

T HE TUDOR GARDEN shared in the whole forward thrust of the 16th century. With the Wars of the Roses in the past, the Englishman could build an undefended, hospitable house and grace it with a garden planned for pleasure as well as for use. He could make it a show-place for entertaining his friends and indulging the Tudor taste for fantastical ornament. He could adopt Renaissance fashions from the Continent and, as the century advanced, he could grow exotic plants introduced from Turkey, the Indies, Mexico and the Americas. If he was an intellectual he could study the new science of botany. If he was an artist he could celebrate flowers in painting or poetry, seeing them not as mystic symbols, but as creations of nature made for our delight.

The Tudor garden was of a good logical shape which stayed in fashion for some hundred and fifty years. It was a square enclosure held in by walls or hedges, sited in front of the house so that house and garden were in friendly unity and the garden could be admired from the front windows or terrace. Inside the square there were usually two main alleys crossing in the centre (as in the old monastery gardens) where there would be an ornament such as a flower-bed or a fountain. There were other parallel alleys, some open and flanked by trained fruit-trees, others covered in by pleached trees to make shady tunnels. Fruit-trees were widely used in the pleasure garden, for the range of flowering shrubs was still small. The alleys were gravelled, sanded, turfed or carpeted with scented herbs, and in the spaces between there were square or oblong flower-beds.

If the owner was old-fashioned, these beds were edged with railings and planted simply, but if he was modish, he would adopt the new style which came in with the century and soon dominated the flower-garden— the knot. This was a bed edged with bricks or low hedges of lavender

or rosemary or (later) with hyssop or box, with a pattern picked out with dwarf plants, coloured gravels and sand. The design was sometimes a formal interlacing pattern, sometimes an animal motif or heraldic emblem—the gardening books of the time were full of patterns to copy. Other features of the garden would be topiary, practised again for the first time since the departure of the Roman legions, trellis arches, and arbours, often with turfed seats inside, as in Chaucer's day. Vegetables and herbs would be grown inside the main square, perhaps tucked behind fruit-trees, and water would either be piped or trundled round in buckets filled from a well and pumped over the plants.

This was the basic, unpretentious garden which might go with a small manor house or a prosperous farmhouse, but of course a rich man's garden was much more elaborate. A large garden would have a mount (or more than one), a small artifical hill with a winding path to the top which stuck up from a flat garden like a boil. There might be banked-up paths inside the boundary walls, sometimes as wide as terraces, so that strollers could walk round looking *down* at the central garden and *out* to the open country. Or there might be covered galleries made of solid 'carpenter's work' leading from the house to the mount or forming a cloister round the garden to protect the aristocratic walker from rain or sun. These wooden galleries were an English speciality. Outside the main pleasure garden there would be space for all sorts of amusements, such as mazes or a bowling-green; English turf was already acknowledged to be the best.

The great men of Tudor England had flamboyant tastes, and no gardens were more sensational than those of Henry VIII, particularly at Hampton Court and Nonsuch (near Ewell in Surrey), designed to dazzle not only the natives but the ambassadors of rival kings abroad.

When Henry took over Hampton Court from Cardinal Wolsey, he enlarged and remodelled the gardens. The basic shape was still a square walled plot but many such plots were put together—the largest for the King, a rose garden for the current Queen, a pond garden, a kitchen garden, an orchard and so on. The King's garden was much cluttered with arbours, statues, mounts, fountains, topiary, sundials, knots, railed beds, aviaries, covered galleries, banqueting pavilions, striped painted seats and bits of nonsense like tall wooden poles with carved heraldic beasts on top, gilded to glitter in the sun.

Nonsuch, of which much is known from documents and excavations though nothing survives intact, was even more of an extravaganza. Henry is said to have sent his gardener to the Continent to study Renaissance ideas and to see François I's Fontainebleau, and Nonsuch was a sort of Franco-Italian hybrid in an English setting. There was a Privy Garden next to the Palace with marble columns, sculptured fountains, falcon perches and beds embroidered with flowers in the latest Italian manner. Beyond was a 'wilderness', a Grove of Diana, a bowling-green, a maze, an orchard and a banqueting house.

The wilderness—a word which now occurs with increasing frequency— was not a wild garden as we know it, but a stage forest with pleached alleys, fruit-trees, clipped evergreens, roses, ferns and wild flowers, with replicas of wild animals dotted among the bushes—a whimsical fancy, but no more so than a modern pond with toads and gnomes. Marble fountains carved with mythical figures poured water from all suitable and unsuitable orifices and there was a water surprise, or booby-trap, to spray the unwary visitor, to delighted roars of laughter, no doubt, from the royal toadies.

A few great lords, such as Lord Burghley, made comparable gardens as the 16th century marched on, with statues, urns and vases in the Italian style. The glory of such a garden would be its sculptured fountains, pouring into pools for bathing or boating. At Lord Burghley's garden at Theobald's, in Hertfordshire, one could go boating among the shrubs.

A large Elizabethan garden must have been a curious hotchpotch of Renaissance splendour with rather childish Tudor twiddles, and was not without its critics at the time. Francis Bacon, in his famous essay *On Gardens* (published in 1625, but possibly written much earlier), condemns statues, knots and fancy topiary, and generally extols the beauty of simplicity. Yet his own ideal garden is far from simple, and includes turrets cut in the hedges with spaces for bird-cages, a trick which even Pliny never thought of. Most garden critics, from Cicero to William Robinson, have complained of artifice while indulging in all sorts of artifice themselves.

Lovers of nature are curiously reluctant to admit that a completely natural garden is a contradiction in terms.

In Jacobean times, the square remained the basic shape, but there were developments. As the fashion for pleasure gardening expanded, a separate kitchen garden was made outside the main enclosure. The Jacobean pundits made a firm distinction between the pleasure garden and the kitchen garden. William Lawson, the author of two charming books published in one volume in 1618, *A New Orchard and Garden* and *The Country Housewife's Garden*, says firmly: 'it is meet that we have two gardens, a garden for flowers and a kitchen garden'. Lawson was a practical Yorkshire man with a gift for communication, a Jacobean Percy Thrower who would have been a television star if he were living today. He told people just what they wanted to know about gardening and his books ran into many editions.

Another change was that the garden tended to move from the front of the house to the back or side. John Parkinson (of whom more will be written later) wrote in 1629 'the four square form is the most usually accepted for all, and doth best agree to any man's dwelling, being (as I said before) behind the house, all the back windows opening into it. Yet if it be longer than the breadth, the proportion of walks, squares and knots may soon be brought into the square form.' In other words, a large garden would consist of many squares and oblongs put together like a puzzle; walled or hedged enclosures might extend round three sides of the house and cover several acres, with avenues, lawns and orchards fitted into the pattern. Raised boundary walks and mounts continued to be fashionable.

Another design development of the 17th century was that the knot was increasingly replaced by the parterre, a parterre being a larger unit, a flat terrace planted with a geometric design of strapwork or writhing scrolls or arabesques. It looked best from above and was rather like a decorated ceiling upside down. The French developed a whole philosophy of parterres, with rules and techniques for different kinds, ranging from the grand *parterre de broderie*, with fantastic patterns picked out in clipped box on a groundwork of sand, charcoal, crushed brick and other coloured materials, with a few flowers or none at all, down to the simple *parterre à l'Anglaise*, of turf cut into patterns and edged with box. An elaborate parterre was a climax of the artificial, a task for the pattern-maker, not the plant-lover.

The square, enclosed style continued through the reign of Charles I and the Commonwealth years until the Restoration, though there were straws in the wind indicating a wish to look beyond the garden walls. Francis Bacon's dream garden was a 12-acre enclosure with an arch giving a view of the cultivated heath beyond; and some of the larger Jacobean gardens introduced flights of steps to give a sense of space and an open view. It cannot be said too often that garden changes are never abrupt. There is always a flow from one style to another; the seeds of a style can be perceived in earlier gardens and the fruits linger long after the style is past its zenith.

But design is only one part of the Tudor and Elizabethan story. Matching the design explosion there was a great expansion of plant knowledge and gardening enthusiasm; there were many new plants to grow and new books to read. Though garden progress comes gradually, there are milestones, and there was one in the middle of the 16th century. In 1551 the first serious English botanist, William Turner, published the first of three parts of an English herbal, in which he looked at plants as a scientist and scholar; instead of accepting tradition and dishing up classical authors, he examined what he saw and looked for proof. His descriptions of flowers are warm and charming, but free of mediaeval mumbo-jumbo. Other herbals followed, culminating in John Gerard's *Herball* of 1597.

Practical gardening manuals were published as well as herbals and sold very well. Thomas Tusser's *Hundred Good Points of Husbandry* (1557) ran into many editions. Written in doggerel verse, it is a book of homely saws about farming, but has a section 'Of Herbs and Flowers' for the housewife, listing herbs for salads and sauces, for physic, strewing and stilling and roots to boil and butter. His advice on 'herbs, branches and flowers for windows and pots' recommends lilies, sweet williams, carnations, lavender, roses and double marigolds, and is perhaps the first English reference to flower arranging. Three years later, a Dutch visitor to

England admired the herbs and nosegays he found in all the rooms of the English home.

More sophisticated than Tusser was Thomas Hill's *The Gardener's Labyrinth* (1577), a best-selling compendium of practical hints, including a how-to-do-it section on the making of a pleached alley and instructions for preserving vegetables. Early editions of these Elizabethan books can be found in botanical libraries and are a joy to read and handle.

The new plants available to the gardener by the end of the century were of two kinds. There were 'improved' varieties of known plants, improved, that is, by selection, and there were introductions from abroad. The big increase in plant material was noted by William Harrison, a country parson and keen gardener who was the H. V. Morton of Elizabethan England; his *Description of England* was first published in 1577. Writing in a second edition ten years later, he says:

> How art also helpeth nature in the daily colouring, doubling, and enlarging the proportion of our flowers, it is incredible to report: for so curious and cunning are our gardeners now in these days that they presume to do what they like with nature, and moderate her course in things as if they were her superiors. It is a world also to see how many strange herbs, plants and annual fruits are daily brought unto us from the Indies, Americas, Taprobane [Ceylon], Canary Isles, and all parts of the world... there is not one nobleman, gentleman or merchant that hath not great store of these flowers.

The newer, rarer plants were of course confined to the gardens of connoisseurs, who must have their own chapter. The run-of-the-mill gardener grew a traditional but increasing range of plants, especially fruit-trees, evergreens, clipping plants, scented plants and small flowers for nosegays. Scent was a much-loved quality in flowers and remained so until the hybridizer brought the rival attractions of great size and bright colour. Privet, thorn, cypress, holly, box, rosemary, juniper, lavender, hyssop and thrift for clipping, and hornbeam, willow and hazel for pleaching, with roses and other climbers to intertwine, were the staples of the 16th-century garden. Lilies, pinks, hollyhocks and all the herbs of the monastic garden would also be cultivated. Thomas Tusser (writing for the ordinary gardener) lists twenty-seven different fruits, and by the end of the century there was a much bigger variety, with cherries and strawberries the favourites. The choicest fruits were still French.

A modest Elizabethan garden must have been a charming spot, with its intimacy, its fine hedges, its fruit blossom, its clipped shrubs, and its mingled scents. The grander gardens must have suffered from the ostentation and pomposity which were to swell large in the following century.

5

TRAVELLERS AND CONNOISSEURS

THE EARLY YEARS of the Elizabethan age saw the dawn of plants-manship, a new English hobby which soon grew into a glorious obsession. No longer concentrating on leeks and onions for the pot or on herbal mixtures for their aches and pains, gardeners were beginning to love flowers for their interest and beauty. They wanted them bigger and brighter and in greater variety.

French, Dutch and Flemish gardeners had for long led the field both as botanists and growers, but the English began to catch up and to develop their own specialities. They were stimulated by a flow of distinguished visitors from the Continent, many of them refugees, and by the end of the 16th century there were cliques of clever gardeners in England botanizing, improving flowers, collecting in person or financing expeditions abroad. With country communications slow and risky, the important centres of gardening activity were the cities, particularly London and its suburbs, where botanists, apothecaries, herbalists, noblemen and merchants met to exchange ideas and plants.

The great Flemish botanist, de l'Obel, was an important capture. He came to England in about 1585, settled here, and in 1606 became King's Botanist to James I. John Gerard, author of the *Herball* of 1597, was another central figure. He was superintendent of Lord Burghley's gardens, including that at his town mansion in the Strand, and had a garden of his own in Holborn where he grew nearly a thousand different plants. Gerard was a chatty and inaccurate herbalist who pinched other men's findings without acknowledgement, but he was a first-rate practical and experimental gardener who infected others with his enthusiasm and wrote exuberant Elizabethan prose. He was a friend of the top botanists of his day, including de l'Obel and Jean Robin, botanist to the King of France

and founder of the Jardin des Plantes. He often went simple-hunting round London with botanically minded cronies, and it is delightful to think of him finding *Osmunda regalis*, or royal fern, on Hampstead Heath and pennyroyal at Mile's End. One of his treasures was ground elder.

A number of noblemen with town houses became patrons of horticulture, like the 11th Baron Zouche, whose botanical garden at Hackney was superintended by de l'Obel, and who is said to have nearly ruined himself with his gardening expenditure; and city merchants, as William Harrison wrote in his *Description of England*, were keen collectors, using their agents abroad and their ships' captains to scour the world for new plants. Some London gardens were large, with room for forest trees as well as choice fruit-trees, trained figs and vines, flowers and shrubs, and a fine supply of vegetables. Tender plants were grown in pots and wheeled into shelter for the winter, notably oranges and lemons, which were very rare in England until well into the 17th century. (Miles Hadfield records that Lord Burghley wrote to Paris in 1562 to order a lemon, a pomegranate and a myrtle to go with his orange-tree—in the singular). Other town gardens were quite small, but then, as today, the size was no measure of the quality. There were town gardens of all dimensions which were treasure-houses of new and rare plants.

From the middle of the 16th century, exotic plants arrived in an increasing flow. Many came from Turkey, for the Turks were great gardeners and had been improving flowers for centuries—introductions from or by way of Turkey included the crown imperial, *Iris susiana*, *I. pallida*, various hyacinths, anemones and narcissi, *Lilium chalcedonicum*, *Muscari moschatum*, *Crocus aureus* and shrubs including *Hibiscus syriacus*, *Philadelphus coronarius* and cherry laurel. Most exciting of all was the first tulip, which came to England in about 1578. The Emperor Ferdinand's ambassador, de Busbecq, had admired the tulips in the gardens of Suleiman the Magnificent and asked for seeds, which he sent home soon after 1554. Other plants came to England from Europe, including *Aster amellus*, *Astrantia major*, the dog's tooth violet, many gladioli, some sea-hollies, new bearded irises, annual candytuft, lavender cotton (an important plant for knots and clipped edgings) and many bulbs. New fruits of the 16th century included gooseberries and apricots and a new vegetable, the Jerusalem artichoke, arrived in 1617.

Wonderful plants came from the New World. The potato was to cause a revolution in food as was tobacco in personal habits. John Gerard planted sugar cane in his garden, which failed, but also bell peppers and sweet corn, which succeeded. He grew the sunflower and *Yucca gloriosa* of North America (his yucca did not flower) and *Mirabilis jalapa*, or marvel of Peru, and got seeds of the Peruvian nasturtium from his friend, Jean Robin. The so-called French and African marigolds, *Tagetes patula* and *T. erecta*, came in from Mexico.

Other plants came, and had come for centuries, by haphazard methods, though little can be proved. Romantics have attributed the hollyhock to the crusaders (who were more likely to have been looting churches than scanning the eastern fields for flowers) and the ivy-leaved toadflax is said to have come to Oxford clinging to Italian statues.

Although our gardeners were still inferior to the Dutch and the French, England had a reputation in Elizabethan times for being prolific in garden forms, especially double flowers, which foreigners attributed to our rainy climate, so that flowers could be selected and replanted all the year round. They gave credit for this to the English housewife, who was increasingly taking charge of the flower garden. Double flowers known by the turn of the century included columbines, daisies, campanulas, buttercups, white primroses, campion, marigolds, cuckoo-flowers, violets, nigella and peonies. Colour variations included a green primrose and red-tinged lily-of-the-valley. Of native flowers newly brought into the garden thrift was of major importance for knots and clipping.

In the first half of the 17th century plantsmanship reached its high noon. English gardeners collected and travelled for plants with an enthusiasm not matched again for decades or even centuries. The more adventurous spirits ranged the world, and the greatest name among them is Tradescant.

There were two magnificent Tradescants, father and son. The father collected all over Europe, in Russia, round the coasts of the Mediterranean and in North Africa; the son explored Virginia and the West Indies, making the first of three voyages in 1637. In the late 1620s the two bought a large house in Lambeth and started a museum and a botanical garden of rare plants. The house became known as Tradescant's Ark and was one of the sights of London, visited by naturalists from all over the world. There were plants of all kinds from rock plants to forest trees, as well as collections of birds, including a dodo, insects, minerals, shells, coins, weapons, fishes, fossils and other curiosities. In about 1630 John I was appointed royal gardener to Queen Henrietta Maria, and was succeeded in the post on his death by his son.

John I's first big assignment as a collector was in 1611, when he was sent to the Continent by the 1st Earl of Salisbury to buy plants for the great country mansion he was building, Hatfield House. The scale of planting at Hatfield was colossal—there were to be thousands of trees for avenues, thousands of vines and bulbs by the ton—and Tradescant's mission was to buy choice stock in Holland and France. In Holland, he bought the most exquisite varieties of fruit-trees, as well as rare roses, tulips, lilies, and scythes and spades, so the Dutch tools must have been better than our own. In Paris he bought more fruit-trees and formed a lasting friendship with Jean Robin.

In 1618, Tradescant was taken on a diplomatic mission to Russia, where he made a pioneer study of Russian flora and collected, among other plants, a single, highly scented rose called *Rosa muscovitica* and a new fringed pink. Soon afterwards he went on a naval expedition to the Mediterranean and a rich harvest of discoveries included new cistuses, roses and narcissi, *Syringa persica*, the Algerian apricot and the Roman peach. Other plants which he later collected or acquired by gift, exchange or purchase (diplomats, merchants and sea-captains were all roped in as collectors) were *Matthiola sinuata*, ancestor of our ten-week stock, *Lobelia cardinalis* (from Jean Robin) and the Virginian spiderwort now known as *Tradescantia virginiana*.

Many of his acquisitions were plants of the New World in which Tradescant and his son were passionately interested—the father bought a 50-acre estate in Virginia as a speculation. Later, when John II went to explore Virginia for himself, he brought back a flood of new exotics. We owe to him many of the treasures of the modern park and garden, forest trees, herbaceous plants and climbers, including the scarlet runner bean. Among his trophies were *Acer rubrum, Platanus occidentalis,* the swamp cypress (*Taxodium distichum*), Virginia creeper (*Parthenocissus quinquefolia*), the trumpet honeysuckle (*Lonicera sempervirens* var. *minor*) and *Mimosa pudica,* collected in the West Indies. These are authentic Tradescant introductions and many others are possible, including the tulip tree (*Liriodendron tulipifera*), *Robinia pseudoacacia,* and *Smilacina racemosa.*

The new exotics were not the only excitement of the flower garden in the Jacobean–Carolean period. The science of horticulture marched ahead. Searching always for new sports and garden forms, gardeners were developing new varieties of known plants so fast that Gerard's *Herball* (1597) seeems a simple affair compared with John Parkinson's *Paradisi in Sole, Paradisus Terrestris* (1629). Gerard named two fritillaries, for instance, a dozen daffodils and two cyclamen, against Parkinson's eleven fritillaries, seventy-eight daffodils and ten cyclamen. Parkinson knew some twenty varieties of ranunculus, some fifty carnations and pinks, many single and double primroses and a huge number of tulips.

The tulip craze was the most sensational horticultural happening there has ever been. Tulipomania reached its height in Holland in the 1630s, when rare bulbs changed hands for prices which might equal a man's whole fortune; a rich man would stake his house or his carriage and pair and a workman his tools, and many went bankrupt when the tulip market crashed. In England, the tulip fashion came later and was more temperate, and the new varieties of tulips and other bulbs were sensibly used to enrich the garden scene.

Parkinson was a London apothecary and his *Paradisus* is a wonderful source of knowledge about both the design and the plants of the early 17th-century garden—Wilfrid Blunt calls it 'perhaps the greatest gardening book in our language'. It covers flowers, vegetables and fruit and is highly practical, with growing instructions, points of identification and flowering dates. But more, it breathes a love of flowers as decoration— Parkinson looks at flowers with seeing eyes. He chose the crown imperial as the first flower in his book. 'The Crown Imperial, for his stately beautifulness, deserveth the first place in this our garden of delight.' He sets great store by double flowers and by scented flowers, which were still prized as in Tudor times. He is discriminating about the wild flowers he collects for his garden, and perhaps despised John Gerard's little weeds:

> The honeysuckle that groweth wild in every hedge, although it be very sweet, yet do I not bring into my garden, but let it rest in his own place, to serve their senses that travel by it, or have no garden. I have three other that furnish my garden, one that is called double, whose branches spread very far, and being fit for an arbour will soon cover it: the other two stand upright, and spread not any way far, yet their flowers declaring them to be honeysuckles, but of less delight, I comfort them with the other.

After the publication of *Paradisus*, Parkinson was given the title by Charles I of *Botanicus Regius Primarius*.

Two other Jacobean dates must be noted as signs of the increasing importance of plants. In 1605, the Gardeners' Company of the City of London, a company for professional nurserymen, was incorporated as a Guild by Letters Patent, and in 1621 the Oxford Botanic Garden was founded, the first botanic garden in Britain, seventy-six years after the first in Europe, at Padua.

6

THE GRAND FRENCH MANNER

AT THE BEGINNING of the 17th century the English garden was a tight enclosure. By the end it had opened out to stretch from the house to the horizon. The garden had burst its walls and merged into the park. The strongest influence was France.

The pace-setter was the King himself. In his years of exile Charles II, who loved gardening, had been dazzled by the architectural perspectives of the French landscape gardeners. He had seen the work of the Mollet family (Claude Mollet had been royal gardener to Henri IV and his three sons rose to equal fame), and probably some of the early work of André le Nôtre, whose first great garden, at Vaux-le-Vicomte, was begun in 1656 and was all but finished in 1661, when the owner, Nicolas Fouquet, held a magnificent fête in honour of the young king Louis XIV, with fireworks, a ballet and a new play by Molière. (Fouquet was arrested three weeks later.) Charles had visions of planting in England, when the time should come, the dramatic avenues, majestic fountains and sumptuous parterres which were the fashion in France.

Other royalist travellers fell under the same influence. The most important to the history of gardening was John Evelyn, who managed to rub along with all political parties and spent most of the Commonwealth years making a garden at Sayes Court, in Deptford. But he knew France and Italy well and had studied French gardens and the great French speciality, the culture of trees, and was soon to launch a hugely successful campaign for more tree planting in England. Space, mathematics and symmetry were the principles of the Restoration garden. The horticulturist, searching his little beds for new forms of dianthus or auricula, gave place to the garden architect whose materials were trees, water and stone.

This book is about trends, and the French style dominated the royal

39

and fashionable world. But gardening trends are never universal, and while many of the great English landlords remodelled their estates in the French style in the second half of the 17th century, there were far more who had no wish to change, or had not the vast sums of money needed, nor the broad acres, while some slow-movers did not hook on to the new fashion for another fifty years, when the *avant-garde* had changed their minds again and were throwing the French style out of the window.

Besides, there were rival influences at work. Gardening had become such a sophisticated art that there was room for opposing styles and dissentient voices. There were great plantsmen and great landscape-architects during the Restoration, and the two gifts cannot be used together. The plantsmen were carrying on from Tradescant and Parkinson, the garden-architects were doing something which, for England at any rate, was new.

Their master was Le Nôtre, who began in the early 1660s to lay out the gardens of Versailles for the Sun King. Le Nôtre gloried in vistas— his gardens could be seen from the upper windows of a palace or château in one sweeping glance. Every Le Nôtre garden had one main axis marching from the house to the horizon, first crossing a parterre, then dividing round a formal lake or canal, then meeting again to pierce tracts of woodland, continuing as far as the eye could see. This main axis would be punctuated with circles or half-moons from which lesser avenues radiated like the points of stars, and in the triangular spaces between were pavilions, fountains, triumphal arches, tracts of water, groves of trees, parterres, statues, mazes, water surprises and other delights.

No garden was made in England on the majestic scale of Versailles, and few gardeners attempted the radiating vistas which worked better in the flat terrain of northern France than among the rolling hills of England. But some bold spirits had a go. Charles II led the way and chose French designs for Hampton Court. (He hoped to bring over Le Nôtre himself but this never came off, although Louis XIV was willing to lend him.) What later became the Great Fountain Garden was begun in Charles's time and was a purely French conception—a semi-circular *patte d'oie*, or goosefoot, on the east side of the palace with radiating avenues of trees,

the middle toe of the goosefoot ending in the Long Water Canal. The King brought over French gardeners for the construction and chose as his royal gardener a man who had studied under Le Nôtre, John Rose.

The richer nobility were not slow to catch on. At Badminton, the 1st Duke of Beaufort cut radiating glades through his woods several miles long, so extensive that the vistas overran his boundaries and he had to persuade the gentry round about to continue the lines through their own land at their own expense. (The Duke of Montagu was less fortunate at Boughton, his neighbour, the Duke of Bedford, refusing to co-operate.) Melbourne Hall, in Derbyshire, was planned as an echo of Versailles. Bramham Park, in Yorkshire, though sadly damaged by the great gale of 1962, is the most nearly perfect French-style park still remaining in England, laid out rather later, in the reigns of Queen Anne and George I. Other French landscapes, now lost, can be found in the highly informative collection of bird's-eye views by Kip from paintings by Knyff, called *Britannia Illustrata*, the first volume of which was published in 1707.

However, a study of Kip suggests that taking England as a whole, the rectangle remained the most important garden shape, particularly in hilly country. The supreme example was Chatsworth. Between 1686 and 1707, Elizabethan Chatsworth was rebuilt in the classical style by the 1st Duke of Devonshire and the gardens were laid out to match by French architects in collaboration with London and Wise, of whom more will be written later. 'Gardens' is too mild a word. A whole countryside was divided into squares and rectangles (no radiations) filled with spectacular features— parterres of unimaginable size, a formal wilderness, a cascade fed from the Derbyshire hills, and magnificent fountains including a copper willow tree which rained from every leaf. The cascade and the Sea-Horse and Triton fountains survive today. Many smaller estates were laid out in the same pattern, formal, open, with oblong parterres and fountains as showy as the landowner's purse allowed. It was an immodest, even bombastic kind of gardening, a vision from France or Italy transposed with variable success to our gentler landscape.

But the French influence was not merely a dream of glory. There was much on the credit side, due largely to the influence of John Evelyn.

From 1660 on, trees were planted in England as never before, particularly after 1664, when Evelyn, a founder member of the Royal Society, published one of the key books of English garden literature, *Sylva, or a Discourse of Forest Trees*. Evelyn's purpose was largely practical. He wanted to promote better estate management and to repair the ravages of the Civil War, and particularly to promote the planting of oaks to ensure a future timber supply for the English navy. *Sylva* is a dullish read today, but it was a contemporary best-seller and was widely followed. Evelyn was a polymath whose many interests included flowers and vegetable gardening, and in 1693 he translated into English La Quintinye's definitive book on fruit, vegetables and orange-trees. La Quintinye was in charge of Louis XIV's *potagers*, the most celebrated fruit and vegetable gardener in history. Most grandees preferred to employ unmarried gardeners, who could presumably work round the clock, but La Quintinye recommended married men, as the wife would be available to clean, scrape and weed, and he favoured the deplorable modern American practice of interviewing both husband and wife when a husband is up for a job. Otherwise, he seems to have been an excellent man.

Hand in hand with tree planting went a boom in evergreen shrubs, especially with gardeners who favoured the Dutch style, which was so popular in England for a number of reasons that it needs a chapter to itself.

To return to the dissentient voices. Two gardening styles, both quite un-French, found followers in the second half of the 17th century. First, the passionate plantsmen continued to love their gardens and to cultivate plants as before. Second, there are exciting signs of the informal, undulating landscape usually associated with the 18th century.

The plantsmen must be traced through literature rather than illustration. Nobody, even to this day, has found a way of illustrating a plantsman's garden. A design can be exquisitely drawn, a flower can be painted or photographed, but a crowded flower-bed must be left to the writer.

One of the most charming of the many gardening books of the Restoration is John Rea's *Flora, Ceres and Pomona* (1665) about flowers, gardens and fruit. This makes it clear that, setting aside the seats of dukes and earls, most gardens were quite small. Rea suggests a garden of 110 yards square for a nobleman (80 for fruit and 30 for flowers) and 60 yards square for a gentleman (40 for fruit and 20 for flowers), all to be surrounded by a brick wall 9 feet high. This is Tudor gardening continued.

He says there must be a stove-house—clearly tender plants and exotic evergreen shrubs like oranges were now in common cultivation. And the range of flowers he discusses show many which are new since Parkinson. He gives enormous tulip lists (a mild form of tulipomania had now hit England), and says wisely that good tulips should be planted alone, preferably one variety to each bed. He is a specialist on rare primroses and double flowers, lists many plants for parterres. He likes birds in the garden, plenty of scent, and flowers even in the vegetable borders. He criticizes the new Frenchified gardens for allowing too little scope for flowers.

Every line by John Rea shows his love of flowers. In a dedicatory verse at the beginning of *Flora*, he says:

> Into your garden you can walk
> And with each plant and flower talk;
> View all their glories, from each one
> Raise some rare meditation.

This is a very English attitude to flowers. One cannot imagine Le Nôtre chatting up his trees.

Rea's book is unillustrated, except for title decorations, for he says illustrations are 'good for nothing, unless to raise the price of the book . . . they are more likely to puzzle or affright the spectator into an aversion, than direct or incite their affections'.

Portents of the natural landscapes of the next century are scarcer, but there are signals. First, there is the introduction of the ha-ha, a link between 'the neat and the rude', usually attributed to Bridgeman in the 18th century, but in fact earlier. The first known ha-ha in England was made in 1694 at Levens Hall, in Cumbria. This garden was laid out by a pupil of Le Nôtre, Guillaume Beaumont, who planned many English estates and almost certainly worked for King William at Hampton Court, so that he came under Dutch influence. His ha-ha at Levens was cut to open up a prospect from the garden to the park. The garden was enclosed, highly formal and thick-planted with topiary in the Dutch manner, but M. Beaumont treated the park in a revolutionary way, planting oaks in clumps and revealing the romantic rocks and cliffs of Whitbarrow. A contemporary critic complained that he was opening up the 'horrid crags'. At Levens, all M. Beaumont's work is still intact—formal garden, topiary, ha-ha, plans, letters and records. This garden has never been restored, having enjoyed an unbroken history, and some of the trees and shrubs growing there today, including some magnificent oaks, are the original plantings. There have been only eight head gardeners since Beaumont himself, most of them living to a great age and each, with the exception of one bad hat, departing life with honour, having passed on his knowledge to his successor.

Another signal is an extraordinary passage in *The Garden of Epicurus*, by Sir William Temple (written in about 1685), in which he reflects on the Chinese landscapes he had never seen:

What I have said, of the best forms of gardens, is meant only of such as are in some sort regular; for there may be other forms wholly irregular, that may, for aught I know, have more beauty than any of the others; but they must owe it to some extraordinary dispositions of nature in the seat, or some great race of fancy of judgment in the contrivances, which may yet reduce some disagreeing parts into some figure, which shall yet, upon the whole, be very agreeable. Something of this I have seen in some places, but heard more of it from others, who have lived much among the Chinese; a people, whose way of thinking seems to lie as wide of ours in Europe, as their country does. Among us, the beauty of building and planting is placed chiefly in some certain proportions, symmetries, or uniformities; our walks and our trees ranged so, as to answer one another, and at exact distances. The Chinese scorn this way of planting, and say a boy, that can tell an hundred, may plant walks of trees in straight lines, and over against one another, and to what length and extent he pleases. But their greatest reach of imagination is employed in contriving figures, where the

beauty shall be great, and strike the eye, but without any order of dis-
position of parts, that shall be commonly or easily observed . . . But I
should hardly advise any of these attempts in the figure of gardens
among us; they are adventures of too hard achievement for any common hands.

Sir William Temple was keeping an open mind. It was a period when
the aristocrat's garden was Frenchified, but elsewhere there was variety
and the play of individual taste, and above all, there was enthusiasm.
In 1691, John Aubrey reported that 'there was now ten times as much
gardening about London as there was in 1660'.

7

THE DUTCH GARDEN

ONCE AGAIN—though for the last time—a major English garden fashion was set by the sovereign. William III and Queen Mary were already knowledgeable and devoted gardeners when they won the English throne, and they continued to make gardens in both England and Holland for the rest of their lives. In England, their most important work was at Hampton Court, where Christopher Wren was commissioned to redesign the East Front and Charles II's *patte d'oie* was elaborated and planted in the Dutch manner, and at Kensington Palace, which King William bought in 1689.

The Dutch style is an offshoot of the French style, and both have their origins in the Italian Renaissance. But Dutch estates were small, the country treeless and cut up by canals, so that the Dutch garden is smaller and more intimate than the French garden, and still water is essential to it. A typical Dutch garden is enclosed, formal, has some sort of canal and at least one fountain.

There were also certain Dutch specialities. The most important was the use of 'greens', which meant a change in the planting of parterres, the cultivation of thousands of evergreen shrubs, and the construction of orangeries and greenhouses to house the tender greens in winter.

The flowery parterres which had developed from the knot were replaced by green parterres of clipped box alone. At Hampton Court, while Wren was working on the new East Front, Charles II's *patte d'oie* was enlarged into the Great Fountain Garden, with thirteen fountains and beds of box scrollwork like rich lace, edged with clipped hollies and yews. At Kensington Palace, London and Wise were commissioned to make a 30-acre garden in the Dutch manner, with a chequerboard of plots of flowers, grass cutwork and box parterres, with a canal and fountains, oranges, lemons and myrtles and many dwarf trees. (The beautiful orangery was built in Queen Anne's reign, in 1705.) Both Hampton Court and Kensington Palace were said by contemporary critics to be so stuffed with box that there was no room to walk, but it was all rooted up by Queen Anne, who disliked both the smell of box and all the works of her late brother-in-law, King William.

The Dutch passion for evergreens had both merits and absurdities. The orange-trees in which the Dutch had long specialized must have looked delightful, grown in tubs on a terrace or bordering a canal. The Dutch were growing excellent oranges in Elizabethan times when in England Lord Burghley was content with his single specimen. By 1650 they were more widely grown in England but were still a luxury, but with William and Mary they became a general fashion. Orangeries were built to house them in winter with large windows to let in the light and stoves to keep out the frost—some of the most delightful buildings, being both functional and ornamental, which have ever graced the garden scene. Other tender evergreens, such as myrtle and oleander, were similarly wheeled indoors for the winter.

Hardier greens, especially box, though known and grown in every country in Europe, were a Dutch mania. (It is curious that so apparently sensible a nation should have gone so hysterical over plants.) Some gardens were grossly overcrowded with topiary and some of the shapes into which the greens were clipped were as ludicrous as those favoured by Pliny. When any fashion reaches an extreme of absurdity there is always a reaction (it was the tight guêpière of the 1950s that provoked the sack dress), and Dutch topiary was soon to be the touchlight for Pope's satire on verdant greens and eventually for the whole landscape movement. In 1713, Pope wrote an essay with a mock catalogue of evergreen sculpture including 'Family Pieces of Men, Women and Children. Any Ladies that please may have their own Effigies in Myrtle, or their Husbands in Hornbeam.' They could also have St George in box, the Black Prince in cypress, an old maid of honour in wormwood, or a topping Ben Jonson in laurel. The Dutch had pushed the pendulum to its extremity, and it had to swing.

There were other Dutch specialities. The *clairvoyée*, or grille gate-in-the-wall, giving a view from the garden of avenues, fountains or country beyond, is usually attributed to the Dutch, and Dutch ornamental gates were of fine design and workmanship. (However, Jean Tijou, who made the great gates at Hampton Court, was a Frenchman.) *Clairvoyées* with open ironwork gates were a feature at Ham House, where internal decorations, furniture and garden, as chosen by the Duke and Duchess of Lauderdale in the 1670s, all show strong Dutch influence. The Dutch also specialized in lead ornaments and sculpture, including lead equestrian statues, and the foremost artist in lead, Jan van Nost, was a Dutchman who had a studio in London. As cultivators of flowers they remained supreme, as the Dutch flower paintings of the 17th and 18th centuries bear witness.

Apart from the personal influence of William and Mary, the Dutch garden had a particular appeal to the English personality. For every English Duke who aspired to emulate the Sun King and look to the horizon there were hundreds of country gentlemen who preferred a more modest style and the privacy of an enclosed garden. Besides, it was easier on the pocket. One simple economy was often ready to hand—a house on an old site might have a moat or fishpond all waiting to be turned into a Dutch canal.

The new demand for evergreen shrubs required intensive propagation and the first great commercial nursery dates from William and Mary, owned by George London and Henry Wise.

London was a pupil of John Rose and went twice to France to see the great new gardens. He became royal gardener to King William and worked on the Great Fountain Garden at Hampton Court and the new gardens at Kensington Palace. With three partners, he started the Brompton Park nursery in 1681 and was joined by Wise in 1687, and the nursery grew to a size of 100 acres. The royal evergreens were wintered there, but took up only a fraction of the total space. The pair soon became celebrated as garden designers as well as suppliers, and they planned and planted gardens all over England for a long period, London riding prodigious distances from one country seat to the next, and Wise running the Brompton nursery. They were consulted on great projects like Longleat,

Chatsworth and Melbourne Hall, and Wise, who was appointed gardener to Queen Anne, in preference to London, was called in to plan the sumptuous parterres at Blenheim.

Their style was French, their point of time the zenith of the formal garden, but they have been included in this chapter because of their fame as nurserymen. Before London and Wise, the nursery trade had been Dutch, but these two cornered it for England. Trees, shrubs, clipped hollies, pyramid yews, fruits, flowers, bulbs, were nurtured in hundreds of thousands at Brompton Park, a few miles west of London, and their fruit catalogue alone makes the modern nurseryman's list look puny—there were 72 varieties of pear-tree! Beautifully packed in osier baskets, the plants went by wagon or, more often, by water. However, the Brompton calendar of flowers lists plants for February to August only, with a few for September. One weakness of the purely formal style is that the garden is a morgue for nearly half the year.

The formal style inspired by France and Holland remained the leading fashion throughout the reign of Queen Anne who died in 1714, just as the wind was changing again.

8

THE LANDSCAPE

THIS TIME the change was fundamental. The formal tradition of many centuries was slowly but surely overthrown, and the 18th century gave birth to a style of gardening which was sinuous and free. The leaders were the intellectuals and the aesthetes—Lord Shaftesbury, Addison, Pope, Lord Burlington, Vanbrugh and Kent spearheaded the landscape movement which became one of the artistic triumphs of English history. All Europe admired it, even the French paying grudging tribute, and it remains one of the wonders of England today. Fortunately, many great landscapes—Rousham, Stowe, Castle Howard, Stourhead, Petworth and others—are still intact or only mildly modified, often in the 18th century itself.

The change did not come with a rush. The protagonists were exceptionally brilliant and articulate men whose theories outran their practice, and the century was more than thirty years old before the fully serpentine landscape came into being. But from the moment when Pope put quill to paper, the formal garden received a mortal blow.

Pope was the fiercest of the early critics of excessive formality. Addison was more reasonable, and, though enjoying the presence of nature in the garden, believed that 'there are as many kinds of gardening as of poetry'. His own garden was 'a confusion of kitchen and parterre', a remarkably tolerant conception for that period.

Pope was not reasonable at all. In an essay in the *Guardian* (1713), he tore the formal style to pieces and thereafter never ceased to extol the beauties of nature and of asymmetry in cross, witty verse and prose. In practice, he was more conservative than he claimed to be. Pope was a brilliant gardener whose advice was widely sought, and he made a garden at his own home at Twickenham with dells, groves and winding paths

as gestures to the natural beauty he admired; but it also had a quincunx and axial walks on the old pattern and the design was quite formal compared with what was to come.

Stephen Switzer, a professional gardener writing at the same period, was another whose practical work was less romantic than his theories. In his *Ichnographia Rustica*, published in 1718, an important and thoughtful book, he said that all art consists in a study of nature, and the garden should be open 'to the unbounded felicities of distant prospect and the expansive volumes of nature herself'. This is not the hard linear prospect of Le Nôtre, with nature subdued by mathematics, but a softer, horizontal landscape, with nature its queen. But Switzer had been a pupil of Henry Wise and his practical work was formal, with terraces, simple green parterres and orange-trees. The 'natural' garden was still largely talk.

There are at least three phases of the landscape in the 18th century, but the principle of all was the same. The ideal was a garden of natural beauty—but every man has his own idea of what natural beauty means.

The early landscapes were transitional. Nobody as yet wanted to abolish the garden altogether. Men wanted to combine a formal but not too fussy garden with a view of an Arcadian scene beyond with winding streams, classical bridges, shady groves, and a romantic suggestion of agriculture—fields of corn and pasture where the shepherds of Virgil's *Eclogues* might have played their pipes and sighed with unrequited love while keeping a casual eye on their sheep. In order to combine the pleasures of a garden and of an open view without having cows and sheep charging into the garden the ha-ha was used as an invisible boundary between the two. (Visible walls or fences keeping sacred nature at bay were now considered an eyesore.) Charles Bridgeman, one of the earliest exponents of this transitional style, retained straight alleys and canals in the garden proper, then surrounded it with a ha-ha so that the garden would melt into the country. Bridgeman was credited by Horace Walpole in his essay *On Modern Gardening* (1770) with inventing the ha-ha, but in fact a few were certainly made before Bridgeman's time.

In about 1715 the first great landscape of which we can trace nearly every step began to be formed at Stowe, where Sir Richard Temple, the first Lord Cobham, called in Sir John Vanbrugh as his architect and Bridgeman as his garden designer. Here Bridgeman made a garden full of straight axes and avenues, but falling far short of French symmetry. There was none of the exact matching of path with path and tree with tree which Pope so detested; there were some natural groves and winding walks. Round the whole went a ha-ha so that the house had a view of the curving hills and open farmlands beyond. First, Vanbrugh, and after his death in 1726, James Gibbs, built temples and pavilions to adorn the garden, of which Vanbrugh's Rotondo is perhaps the most beautiful. (Its hemispherical dome, of pure geometric conception, was later altered by Borra, giving it gentler curves to suit the new gentler landscape.)

Both Switzer and Bridgeman were men who looked at nature with their own eyes, admiring England's beautiful landscape with direct glance. But in the decade when Stowe was in the making (the first years of George I's reign) there dawned a far more complicated vision. Landscapists arrived who did not see nature directly with the naked eye, but indirectly, through the eyes of painters, particularly Claude and Poussin, the French landscape painters of the previous century who had painted the serene Italian countryside with its lovely legacy of classical temples, ruins, columns and aqueducts. For this the 3rd Earl of Burlington and his protégé, William Kent, who was a (bad) painter before he became an architect, were largely responsible. Burlington went to Italy in 1714 and was thunderstruck. Five years later he and Kent travelled in Italy together and when they returned Kent went to live in Burlington House, and stayed there for life. These two saw all art in Italian terms, though the architecture and the landscapes they admired were of different periods—the architecture of Palladio and the landscapes of ancient Italy. Their combined influence on the shaping of England was incalculable.

It is sometimes said that the paintings of Claude and Poussin *created* the English landscape, but this is almost unbelievable, a misunderstanding of how an artistic movement comes into being—certainly an undervaluing of the English creative achievement. It is much more likely that the landscape movement was well under way when its designers seized on the

Italian theme and used it to enrich their work. Whichever is true, it is certain that the English landscape garden became a conscious picture, with the countryside treated as a canvas; and it had literary as well as pictorial associations, for Claude and Poussin were themselves looking back to the Latin pastoral poets and often painted Virgilian scenes. In some landscapes there is yet a third element, a philosophical theme, particularly in the estates of the great Whig families, and temples to admired principles, such as Liberty, matched the freedom of the design.

The first true pictorial landscape which can be seen intact today is one of the loveliest of all, made by Kent at Rousham on the River Cherwell at some time in the 1730s. Here, in the comparatively small space of 25 acres, Kent made an exquisite idealized Italian country scene with winding walks, a lovely interplay of light and shade, informal water, and classical arcades and statues perfectly placed among the groves and glades. The Vale of Venus, the Temple of Echo, Praeneste, statues of gods, nymphs, satyrs and a Dying Gaul echo in both words and shapes the Italy of the Augustan age.

Pope, in his famous *Epistle to Lord Burlington* (1731), summed up with characteristic clarity the pictorial quality of the new kind of garden:

> Consult the genius of the place in all;
> That tells the waters or to rise or fall.
> Or helps th' ambitious hill the heavens to scale,
> Or scoops in circling theatres the vale,
> Calls in the country, catches opening glades,
> Joins willing woods, and varies shades from shades,
> Now breaks, or now directs, th' intending lines;
> Paints as you plant, and, as you work, designs.

We have come a long way from Switzer's view of a useful, natural garden. Palladian bridges spanning English streams, classical arcades overlooking English farmland, ruined temples nestling in the folds of English hills are not masterpieces of nature, but of sophisticated art.

Unfortunately, when something as revolutionary as the landscape movement comes along, much that is beautiful and valuable is destroyed.

The Landscape

Many straight avenues of fine trees fell to the axe, many simple canals were bent to sinuous lines, many fountains were abolished in favour of waterfalls, many flower gardens were dug over. The Great Parterre at Blenheim, planted by Henry Wise, was abolished by Lancelot Brown, a priceless piece of history lost. Sir William Chambers later complained (1772) that whole woods had been swept away 'to make room for a little grass and a few American weeds'.

As the movement gathered pace, other motifs challenged the dominance of all things classical. Some landscapists, including Kent himself, adopted Gothic ornament, and Gothic follies and towers sprang up in the scenery, with ruins and dead trees to add to the mood of pleasant melancholy. Sometimes—the *reductio ad absurdum* of picturesque detail—there was a hermitage with a real live hermit, though suitable candidates for the job were not easy to find. Other designers preferred the Chinese style. Sir William Chambers, architect of the pagoda at Kew, had visited China as a young man and became an enthusiast for oriental gardening, with its series of arranged scenes and surprises. But only recently has the full extent of the oriental fashion been fully understood with the discovery of a lost landscape painter, Thomas Robins, whose heyday was in the middle of the century. Robins's elegant rococo paintings of real, named houses show, not merely chinoiserie details in an English landscape, but whole houses and their gardens orientalized to make Chinese pictures. Façades with upturned eaves, Chinese gothic pavilions and gates, bamboo bridges, fretted palings and artificial hills and ponds combine to make 'picturesque' landscapes with a vengeance.

The second phase of the landscape movement is marked by the arrival of Lancelot or 'Capability' Brown. Capability Brown is a name to conjure with today, and any threat to a Brown landscape meets strong opposition. Brown was gardener at Stowe from 1741 to 1751, probably starting under Kent, but in 1751 he set up on his own as a consultant and 'improver', and was so popular over the next thirty years that he designed or adapted more than two hundred estates. But even before his death in 1783 his work found some virulent critics. Gardening may seem a gentle occupation, but it rouses passions as hot as the passions of religion or politics.

Brown made the landscape simpler and barer. He abolished the garden, swept the lawn right up to the house, and used as his materials the contours of the site, turf, water and trees. He did not care for temples and statues or the other pictorial features of his predecessors, and indeed destroyed many in redesigning the estates of his clients. (He did a hatchet job on the waterworks at Chatsworth, where the 4th Duke of Devonshire was romanticizing his classical estate.) His landscapes were a slice of the English countryside with clumps of trees, hills and fields, lakes and streams, arranged in quiet harmony. The late Christopher Hussey wrote somewhat harshly, 'I do not think he was particularly sensitive to visual impressions', but thought he had a literary mind. Brown admittedly thought of trees as punctuation marks (which perhaps suggests not so much a literary man as a typographer), and his clumps, usually of hardwood trees, but sometimes of firs or larches with an occasional cedar, were his signature. Their merit was their simplicity, at a time when design was turning into tricksiness, and when nobody could walk through a garden without having his thoughts dictated to him. Here you must think of Horace (Sabine farm scene), here of the virtues of freedom (a temple to Liberty), here reflect on death (a mausoleum). The failure of Brown's landscapes was two-fold—they were thin on plant interest and they could be considered dull.

In a Brown landscape garden the house rises isolated in a sea of grass with flowers and vegetables far away out of sight, so that there is no interest whatsoever for the plantsman; even his lakes had no water plants at the verges, nothing but grass. And his landscapes were monotonously similar—always a surrounding belt of trees, clumps, rolling pasture, and water in the middle distance, often ending in real or dummy bridges —'home-brewed rivers that Mr Brown makes with a spade and a watering-can' said Horace Walpole. His finest surviving work is at Blenheim, where he made twin lakes under Vanbrugh's triumphal bridge, with a tree-covered island and cascades.

Brown's work was criticized more fiercely after his death by two gentlemen from Herefordshire, Sir Uvedale Price and Richard Payne Knight, who wanted wilder, more romantic scenery than either Brown or his successor, Humphry Repton, provided—picturesque gardens in the modern sense of the word. But their writings carry one into a side-stream of aesthetic criticism beyond our scope. Price, in particular, seems to be labouring away about nothing.

Humphry Repton (1752–1818) is the chief author of the third landscape phase, and his entry is very welcome, for he brought back the garden. He is the bridge between the moody 18th-century landscape and the early Victorian garden, with its ideal of education and usefulness. He moved away from the 'painted' scene, reintroduced terraces, flower-beds and rose gardens near the house, clothed the house walls with climbers, revived the trellis-walk, the conservatory and the shrubbery, and believed that the house must make a unity with the garden, not be just a hunk of architecture in a park. He was as successful an improver as Capability Brown had been, but he gave his clients more individual attention. He produced a Red Book—a portfolio of notes and before-and-after sketches bound in red morocco—for every project. His Red Books show that he was quite a canny salesman. He often sketched a garden *before* improvement in the depths of stormy winter, while the same garden *after* improvement was shown in glorious sunshine, with the family eating *al fresco* under a tree.

Repton was parodied by Peacock in a great comic passage in *Headlong Hall* which begins 'I perceive,' said Mr Milestone, after they had walked a few paces, 'these grounds have never been touched by the finger of taste.' And Jane Austen made good-humoured fun of him in *Mansfield Park*, where the rich, oafish Mr Rushworth wants his country place improved.

'Your best friend upon such an occasion,' said Miss Bertram calmly, 'could be Mr Repton, I imagine.'

'That is what I was thinking of. As he has done so well by Smith, I think I had better have him at once. His terms are five guineas a day.'

Anybody who wishes to study the unfolding of the landscape movement from its youth to its maturity, in its varying moods and with its several motives, can find the essence in a single place by visiting Stowe. Many of the greatest designers worked there—Vanbrugh, Bridgeman, Kent,

Gibbs and Capability Brown, each adding to the work of his predecessors rather than destroying it (though Vanbrugh lost some pyramids), perhaps because the true creators of Stowe were the Temple family themselves (followed by the Grenvilles), who refused to be pushed about by architects, but were masters in their own domain. The early garden of Bridgeman, formal but stretching open arms towards the pastoral landscape beyond, with its buildings by Vanbrugh and Gibbs, was the garden which Pope admired in 1731.

> Nature shall join you, time shall make it grow
> A work to wonder at—perhaps a Stow.

By the end of Bridgeman's time, in 1734, the garden was some 60 acres in size. Soon after this date, Kent went to work and expanded the garden both in size and scope, developing Stowe into the ultimate expression of the philosophical garden, a much larger landscape with a Temple of Ancient Virtue, a statue to Comedy and a Temple of British Worthies in a lovely valley called the Elysian Fields. The garden was now rich in exquisite buildings of which more than thirty remain today. In a year of drought, a lucky visitor may see even further into the past if he stands on the steps of the South Front, where he will distinguish a criss-cross of straight lines of grass much greener than the rest of the burnt-up lawns, and a broad green ribbon stretching into the distance—the ghost of the old 17th-century parterre.

And what about the gardeners of this century who did not have hundreds of acres to landscape—the townsmen, the parsons, the minor gentry? They maintained their interest in horticulture and grew an increasing variety of flowers, vegetables and fruit, but they were not unaffected by the movement. A shrubbery, specimen trees or well-placed clumps of trees, possibly a ha-ha even in quite a small garden, and a general loosening up of garden design reflected the influence of Kent and his successors.

It was a good century for botany. The Apothecaries' Garden in Chelsea flourished under the great gardener and author of *The Gardeners Dictionary* (1731), Philip Miller, and was visited in 1736 by Linnaeus, who thought highly of the Dictionary, which Miller later re-edited using the Linnaean binomial system of nomenclature. It ran into many editions. Chelsea was soon to be succeeded in importance by Kew Gardens, where the widowed Princess Augusta laid the foundations of the great garden of today. The first gardening periodical, *The Botanical Magazine*, was published in 1787. Towards the end of the century, experiments began in a revolutionary method of propagating plants by hybridization, which was to wax stronger in the following century, and to be expounded by Darwin in 1876.

Specialists who were not botanists but exhibition growers, known as florists, also contributed to the development of flowers. The first half of the 19th century was the florists' heyday, but growing for the show bench was already an intense pursuit in the 18th century: it had its origins in France and Flanders and had been introduced by refugees. In 1790, eight kinds of flowers were being grown for exhibition—hyacinths, tulips, ranunculus, anemones, auriculas, carnations, pinks and polyanthus.

Ever more plants came from abroad, as seeds, growing plants or dried specimens, especially from North America and South Africa, and from Australia and New Zealand after Captain Cook's voyage in the *Endeavour*, which set out in 1768 carrying on board a rich, brilliant young botanist called Joseph Banks.

9

THE GARDENESQUE

WITH the industrial revolution, new fortunes were made in manufacturing which began to overtake the wealth of the landed gentry, particularly in the north of England. The essentially patrician landscape ceased to be the most fashionable garden and a new middle-class style grew up, a true gardener's garden, rather hideously called the gardenesque. John Claudius Loudon was its most distinguished champion, the period of his fame being from about 1806, when he was only twenty-three, until his death in 1843, though his influence lingered for long.

Loudon was a high-minded Scotsman of gritty courage and demonic industry. He was a born gardener whose greatest pleasure as a child was to work the little plot which his father, a Lanarkshire farmer, had given him. His wife later related that when an uncle in the West Indies sent the family a present of a jar of tamarind, John Claudius let the other children have his share of the fruit provided they gave him the seeds.

He had a passion for self-improvement and supplemented the good education he was given in Edinburgh with extra classes and private study, and was an indefatigable scholar all his life. Though not a natural linguist, he later taught himself French and Italian, and then studied Hebrew and Greek, as well as science, botany and agriculture; he was interested in every kind of mechanical invention, particularly in the scientific management of hot-houses. But self-education was not enough. His aim was to disseminate gardening information far and wide, to promote the kind of gardening he admired, and to improve the living standards of the working gardener. He was lucky enough to marry in 1831 a much younger but equally gifted wife, Jane, a novelist and writer who re-edited his work after his death, updating it, with the help of advisers, with far more success

than usually accompanies these marital acts of homage. This couple, with their moral and educational aims, seem typical of the reforming giants of the Victorian age, though in fact Loudon was already famous during the Regency and died a few years after Queen Victoria came to the throne.

Loudon practised for a short time as a landscape gardener while still in his early twenties and made a great deal of money (which he later lost). But in 1806 he caught rheumatic fever and suffered appalling ill-health for the rest of his life, at one time having to have his right arm amputated. So he transferred his driving energy to writing and produced a torrent of didactic books, articles and pamphlets, mostly with titles too long to quote. They were well written, scholarly and immediately successful. In 1822, he brought out a monumental *Encyclopaedia of Gardening*, still an essential reference book, the fruit of enormous reading and of travels all over Europe and Russia, where, in spite of bad health, he left no botanist unvisited, no interesting garden unseen in country after country. In 1826 he started the *Gardener's Magazine* as an outlet for his opinions, airing all his hobby-horses—self-education, the need for gardening libraries, the mismanagement of the Horticultural Society of London, and cottage economy. So cogent was his style that a number of the landed gentry were persuaded to remodel the dwellings of their gardeners and farm workers. Between 1833 and 1838 he published his *magnum opus*, an eight-volume study of native trees and shrubs called *Arboretum et Fruticetum Britannicum*, and in 1836 a book which concerns us more closely here, *The Suburban Gardener and Villa Companion*, aimed chiefly at the well-to-do middle class; it is the gospel of the gardenesque.

Here Loudon analyses what he calls First, Second, Third and Fourth Rate Gardens, ranging from the garden of a large estate down to that of a terraced house in a street, but one feels that the medium gardens of from one to three acres belonging to the villas of the new industrial suburbs are those nearest to his heart.

Loudon's garden still holds echoes of the romantic period. It is irregular, with winding paths and pretty decorations such as rockwork or rustic arches. But basically, it is a useful, instructive garden, subdued in colour, a haven for interesting plants, 'a garden for displaying the art of the gardener.'

The design of the garden is simple. The house is clothed with climbers, preferably evergreens, and has a conservatory attached. It opens on to a terrace decorated with evergreen shrubs, urns or statues, *but not too many of them*. The gardenesque is not a crowded style. A straight or winding path leads down to a lawn with scattered flower-beds, and continues to some interesting point in the garden such as a fountain, summerhouse or rockery. Rockeries were increasingly popular, ranging from piles of small stones to towering imitations of Mont Blanc or the Matterhorn.

The innovation is the separatist use of plants. Each plant is seen individually, so that plants must never touch each other. Each must be skilfully grown and trimmed to perfect shape so that every one is worthy of careful examination. Plants of medium size are placed singly in small flower-beds in the lawn. Trees and shrubs are grown either singly or in groups, but even when in groups there must be air between. So the shrubbery in which the early-Victorian young lady walked with her admirer would not be a bosky thicket providing welcome concealment from prying eyes, but quite a scattered planting. Beyond the garden there was often a pinetum planted with separated specimens of conifers, including the new discoveries from North America.

Since all the plants were to bear individual scrutiny, they must not be banal, and Loudon pressed for the planting of exotics, rarities and plants which are difficult to grow, especially the new plants which were pouring in from all over the world. He wanted the maximum of variety in the garden and thought that a native plant was never as good as a foreign one. Of course many foreign plants are tender or half-hardy in England, but as greenhouse heating by the circulation of hot water instead of by fires and flues came in in the 1830s, his love of tender plants was easily gratified.

From Loudon's long, full plant lists one can select only a few of special interest. Of trees, he commended many conifers, including the new introductions which that unhappy, doomed collector, David Douglas, was sending home from the Pacific coast of North America. He loved fleshy-leaved evergreens, like magnolias, rhododendrons, camellias, laurels. The exotic spikiness of yuccas was perfect for single planting in small round flower-beds. Weeping trees were ideal for specimen positions. Conifers were displayed in lawns or in large tubs or pots. Roses had their place, as standards or in baskets or climbing over rustic arches, but not mixed in with other plants. Bedding plants like pelargoniums or fuchsias must be planted in groups of one of a kind, and must not be overcrowded. The gardenesque, though it is a stiff, prim way of gardening, is none the less a plantsman's style. The plant is not subjugated to architecture or design but controls it, and it is interesting that William Robinson, who later led the return to 'natural' gardening, was an admirer of Loudon and dedicated the first volume of *The Garden* to his memory. The gardenesque, calling as it does for plant knowledge, scientific study and general self-improvement, was a forerunner of similar Victorian attitudes in other fields.

A delightful picture of gardenesque planting can be found in Disraeli's high-flown romantic novel, *Lothair*; written in 1870, it describes a park planted in about 1800 with all the trees as specimens, no longer in the belts and clumps of Capability Brown:

'... My Lord has ordered the char-a-banc, and is going to drive us all to Chart, where we will lunch,' said Lady St Jerome; ''tis a curious place, and was planted only seventy years ago by my Lord's grandfather, entirely with spruce firs, but with so much care and skill, giving each plant and tree ample distance, that they have risen to the noblest proportions, and with all their green branches far-spreading on the ground like huge fans.'

It was only a drive of three or four miles entirely in the park. This was a district that had been added to the ancient enclosure; a striking scene. It was a forest of firs, but quite unlike such as might be met with in the north of Europe or of America. Every tree was perfect, huge and complete, and full of massy grace...

They sate down by the great trees, the servants opened the luncheon baskets, which were a present from Balmoral. Lady St Jerome was seldom seen to greater advantage than distributing her viands under such circumstances. Never was such gay and graceful hospitality. Lothair was quite fascinated as she playfully thrust a paper of lobster sandwiches into his hand, and enjoined Monsignore Catesby to fill his tumbler with Chablis.

With the return of the serious flower garden and the arrival of the botanically interesting pinetum there came a revival of the vegetable garden, which had been banished by the landscape men to some obscure and distant corner of the estate. As a vivid witness of the pleasures of vegetable gardening we have no less a personality than that great and good man, William Cobbett, who wrote a witty but practical book called *The English Gardener* in 1829. Cobbett found the kitchen garden an object of beauty and delight—'to watch the progress of the crops is by no means unentertaining to any rational creature'—and recommended that it should be alongside the house. He pointed out that it was absurd for people to have imitation fruit on the chimney piece while shunning the sight of a living fruit-tree.

He said that a small, intensively cultivated plot would produce more than would a large area with empty spaces. He had an ingenious idea for keeping out garden thieves (characteristically, he was unwilling to prosecute them)—a thorny hedge and a deep ditch outside the garden wall which could only be stormed by scaling ladders. He had strong views on manure, preferring ashes, lime, chalk, rags, salt and composts to dung, which he said made vegetables coarse and gross. His theories about cultivation were ninety per cent right in the light of modern knowledge, but sometimes quirky. He loved chalk soil and said 'no tree rejects chalk', which is clearly nonsense. But in spite of occasional spasms of cussedness, Cobbett stands squarely for the new gardening common-sense.

Throughout the pre-Victorian and early Victorian period, much gardening news comes from the north of England and the midlands. At the top end of the scale, there was the great new garden at Chatsworth, a product of the age of new techniques and plant introductions. Here the 6th Duke of Devonshire, aided by his brilliant gardener-engineer, Joseph

Paxton, formed the garden we see today with its arboretum and pinetum and sensational Emperor fountain throwing a jet 300 feet high in the glorious setting of the Derbyshire hills, though, tragically, Paxton's masterpiece has gone, the Great Conservatory, begun in 1836 and built on the same engineering principles as the later Crystal Palace of 1851. In this spectacular building the Duke and Mr Paxton reared new and marvellous tropical plants and made a collection of orchids, and here the royal water lily, *Victoria amazonica*, a plant of shameless size with leaves like big round tea-trays, flowered for the first time in England in 1849.

More modest events, too, centred in the north and the midlands, for it was there that the florists' clubs run by factory workers and artisans, usually centred on a local pub, were most lively. The show polyanthus of Sheffield, the Paisley pink, the pansies of the Derbyshire miners, the auriculas of the Lancashire cotton workers, reached a rare perfection. Fuchsias, dahlias, geraniums, and other flowers joined the original florists' *élite*. Miles Hadfield tells us in his *History of British Gardening* that the Paisley operatives brought their delicate touch in the making of muslins to the cultivation of exquisite pinks. He adds that the Florists' Club in Paisley was 'notable for its peacefulness and sobriety'.

Other outstanding events of the period were the founding of the Horticultural Society of London in 1804, which was later to become the Royal Horticultural Society; a great development in the cultivation of roses, perhaps inspired by the Empress Josephine's garden at Malmaison and by the beauty of the rose paintings of her protégé, Redouté; and the first burst of 19th-century plant introductions, the conifers of David Douglas, which transformed English gardens in the middle of the century—for better or worse.

Douglas was another Scot, but, unlike Loudon, he was fundamentally an unhappy man, uneasy in society yet lonely in the wilds. Born in 1799, he spent the best years of his short life collecting plants on the almost unknown west coast of North America, with Indians for guides and a dog as his dearest companion. His hardships are almost unbearable to read about; on one occasion he lost his whole collection of plants in a flood and on another the party were so hungry that they had to eat his specimen berries. He died in 1834 in Hawaii having fallen, while collecting plants, into a bull-pit, where a wild bull tore him to pieces.

Many plants bear his name or carry his memory, including the pretty little annual butter-and-eggs plant, *Limnanthes douglasii*. But it is as a collector of conifers that he made his mark. He sent home so many new species of pine and fir that he once wrote to Dr Hooker at Kew 'You will begin to think that I manufacture pines at my pleasure!'

10

HIGH VICTORIAN

THE FADING LIGHT of romanticism which still tinged the garden-esque did not last long. The curse of mass production put a blight on gardening in about the middle of the 19th century, bringing rigidity of design and garish planting. Communications in England were now so good that fashion was more pervasive than in any previous century, and the new vulgarity charmed and excited gardeners of every class. Two fuses set the fashion alight—the improved greenhouse and the mass of new exotics which collectors were sending home from all over the world. The spirit which built the Empire inspired societies and commercial firms, even individual aristocrats and tycoons, to send botanical expeditions to the Himalayas and the jungles of Asia and South America, and their prizes were rich.

The high Victorian garden was brilliant in colour, far brighter than any earlier English garden which had to depend largely on hardy plants. India, Mexico, Brazil, Peru, South Africa sent their jewels to be nursed under glass in winter and to blaze forth in summer out of doors. Every rich man now had a row of greenhouses and a large staff of gardeners and by heaven, he was going to make it plain that he could grow ten thousand half-hardy plants every year without losing a wink of sleep over the bills.

When the greenhouses were full to bursting point, where were the exotic plants to go? Into parterres, geometric beds and ribbon borders in hectic displays of carpet bedding. Large gardens had to be re-laid out in a suitable style to accommodate the jigsaws of sunny beds and an Italia-nate style was widely adopted—not the cool, graceful formal style of earlier centuries, but a mechanical revival with vast stereotyped terraces and flights of steps, massive statues and fountains, balustrades loaded with

urns of bedding plants. Statuary was now mass produced like everything else, and could unfortunately be provided in unlimited quantity. The best-known architects of the neo-Italian garden were William Nesfield, Sir Joseph Paxton and Sir Charles Barry, and it is almost impossible for the modern eye to enjoy their terraces and parterres, so totally lacking in poetry. A folio book illustrating the new gardens of the mighty was published in 1858 by a fine lithographer called E. Adveno Brooke, and one is stunned by the ostentation he reveals. The Prince Consort himself laid out the grounds of Osborne, Queen Victoria's favourite home, in the same manner.

Small gardens were equally affected by the bedding craze, and even a workman's terraced house would have its mosaic beds cut out of the front lawn, crammed with orange, scarlet, purple, yellow, blue and white bedding plants, plain, spotted and striped. In fact, bedding schemes look much better on this scale than in showy masses. The poorer man might buy his plants from one of the new nurseries which were springing up everywhere, or from a hawker with a barrow, or he might raise them himself in a lean-to greenhouse or even in a glass porch, a sensible custom still widely followed in the north of England. One of the few pockets of resistance to carpet bedding was the country cottage, and it was from the gardens of cottages, parsonages and farmhouses that many old-fashioned perennial plants which had been almost lost to cultivation were rescued when the reaction set in in the 1880s.

Brilliance of colour was the top requisite of the mid-Victorian garden. (At exactly the same time, fabrics became brighter than ever before, with the discovery of aniline dyes.) Many writers described gardens 'blazing with colour', 'of startling brilliance', 'kaleidoscopic with calceolarias', and 'blazing with flower beds of every hue'. Disraeli and Mrs Ewing are excellent sources, the former intoxicated with the gay parterres, the latter horrified and saddened by them. Both biennials and half-hardy annuals were used in the bedding schemes, conspicuous among them calceolarias, lobelias, geraniums (pelargoniums), heliotrope, begonias, French and African marigolds, *Salvia splendens*, fuchsias and zinnias. Usually there was a spring display of bedding bulbs and the main display followed in July and lasted until the autumn frosts, when presumably the rich Victorians returned to their town houses.

It was not only the parterres and ribbon beds which flamed with colour. The dull green shrubberies of Jane Austen, with their privets and aucubas, acquired a glow as new shrubs were imported, particularly the wonderful rhododendrons from the Himalayas which were being collected in hundreds by Joseph Hooker, one of the most successful collectors in history. In 1847 Hooker, who was the younger son of Sir William Hooker, Director of Kew Gardens, left for India under the auspices of Kew and for two years explored, collected and surveyed in Sikkim and eastern Nepal, climbing to heights of over 19,000 feet, and then continued in Bengal. He collected between 6,000 and 7,000 plant species, especially rhododendrons in a vast range of sizes and colours, sending chests of plants and seeds home whenever transport was available. When he returned to England in 1851 he had the joy of seeing many of his seeds already growing up in the Kew nurseries.

Other Victorian collectors combed the world from Chile to China and—one of the last countries to be cracked open—Japan. William Lobb, Robert Fortune, John Gould Veitch were among the most distinguished. The conservatory became as brilliant as the parterre as the tropics yielded their treasures, especially the orchids of South America and south east Asia. New orchids were found in quantity and were highly prized, but sadly, orchid hunters became so competitive that some habitats were almost stripped of their flowers.

There was one department of the Victorian garden which was not ruled by colour. The Victorians, including, of course, the Queen and the Prince Consort, had a passion for conifers, and grew them singly or in avenues or pineta. Wellingtonias and monkey puzzles, Douglas firs and Japanese cedars, Sitka spruces, the Monterey cypress, were eagerly sought as soon as introduced, and gave interest, though of a sombre kind, to the garden in winter. One garden and park at Elvaston Castle, in Derbyshire, the seat of the Earl of Harrington, were entirely stocked with evergreens, both native and rare. Evergreen hedges, parterres, shrubberies and woodlands must have made a gloomy picture, a backdrop for a sinister fairy story.

Another green fashion was for leafy conservatory and house plants, and palms, ferns, aspidistras and ivies filled the winter garden or sprouted from wire baskets or china jardinières in Victorian drawing-rooms. Most of these plants were exotics. Native plants and old-fashioned perennial plants had a hard time to survive until the rescue parties came in 1880.

11

THE PARSONAGE GARDEN

THE TRADITION of the country priest as a gardener has very ancient roots, for the village parson always lived off the land, often, in the lean centuries, working in the fields as a peasant. From Queen Anne's reign onward, as his property and status increased, he became a natural leader in most country pursuits, and having more education and a better library than any of his parishioners, would tend to have the best garden in the village. A vast number of the renowned gardeners and naturalists of the 18th and 19th centuries were parsons, which is not surprising when you consider how many younger sons took Holy Orders as a matter of course.

The parson, riding, walking or driving about his parish, had every opportunity for observing nature, and although naturalists are not always gardeners, the two interests tend to go together. The best-loved naturalist of all, Gilbert White, curate of Selborne, kept a *Garden Kalendar* which is quite as knowledgeable in its way as the more famous *Natural History and Antiquities of Selborne.* In beautiful, legible handwriting, he recorded the planting, cultivating and cropping of his garden for twenty years from 1751 to 1771, not forgetting to notice the weather and the pests. He took a keen interest in the design of his garden, his taste being 'transitional', with old-fashioned flower-beds near the house, but a ha-ha and specimen trees beyond in the newer 18th-century manner. He grew an enviable range of fruit and vegetables, and there was scarcely a delicacy which did not grace his table—asparagus, seakale, cucumbers, broccoli, melons and many varieties of beans and peas. George Crabbe, the poet, was another gardening parson of the period, specializing in grasses and the rarer native plants, rather than 'showy foreigners'.

It is often said that the country parson was a good gardener because he had plenty of leisure, but this is questionable. Certainly a rich, easy-going parson in the 18th century would have had time to spare from his parish for sporting or scholarly pursuits—for fox-hunting, shooting, farming, whist, dancing, diary-keeping, letter-writing, archaeology, botany, entomology or gardening, according to his tastes. But when you get to the reformed and reforming parsons of the Victorian age, their output of work was strenuous, and gardening had to be fitted in with social work, politics, theological controversy and, nearly always, with deep involvement in the founding, fund-raising and teaching of the village school.

Even so, the roll of 19th-century parsons who were outstanding gardeners is impressive. Among the giants were the Rev. the Hon. William Herbert, Rector of Spofforth, Yorks, later Dean of Manchester, known as the pioneer of English hybridizing and expert on the family Amaryllidaceae; by 1823 he had produced thirty new varieties of hippeastrum by cross-breeding; the Rev. John Stevens Henslow, who was energetic in his parish of Hitcham, Suffolk, but was also a brilliant Professor of botany at Cambridge; the Rev. C. A. Johns of Cornwall, wild-flower man rather than gardener, but author of the classic *Flowers of the Field* from which many modern gardeners learned their first lessons—it was one of Miss Jekyll's three favourite books; Dean Hole, Vicar of Caunton, Notts, and later Dean of Rochester, fox-hunter, *bon viveur* and driving spirit behind the National Rose Society; the Rev. J. H. Pemberton, famous hybridizer of roses; and the Rev. William Wilks, Rector of Shirley in Surrey and Secretary of the Royal Horticultural Society, to whom we owe the Shirley poppies. John Keble and Charles Kingsley were not perhaps among the giants, but they were keen practitioners.

The rectory or vicarage garden of middle to late Victorian times was often quite a show-place. Many parsons were reasonably well-to-do—Trollope's starving perpetual curates were an unlucky minority—and could certainly afford a gardener and perhaps a gardener's boy as well. The average garden was from one to three acres in size, including the paddock, with the parish church as its background. It was well stocked and well kept, with the fruits of continuity in the form of mature trees and fine lawns for garden parties, croquet, archery or tennis. The garden had a

settled look, for many parsons, having found a comfortable living, were happy to stay in the same village for life, and it was often the home of new and rare plants, the parson being far more likely than the squire or anyone else in the village to be a plant connoisseur. Loudon's *Encyclopaedia* (Jane Loudon's revised edition), which has a formula for every conceivable aspect of gardening, said that the plant range of the parsonage garden should be as wide as possible, that fanciful prettiness should be avoided, and that there should be some solid evergreen trees to harmonize with the yews and cypresses of the churchyard. This function was often fulfilled by a cedar of Lebanon, a tree introduced in the 17th century. Loudon himself thought that a parsonage garden should have small plots where children could learn to dig and plant.

One might take as the ideal of the Victorian parsonage garden that of Canon Ellacombe, Vicar of Bitton in Gloucestershire, a great scholar and plantsman, the friend of William Robinson, E. A. Bowles, W. J. Bean, Ellen Willmott, and nearly all the great English gardeners of the late 19th and early 20th centuries. Born in 1820, he died in 1916 at the age of ninety-six, gardening to the last. His father, another master gardener who lived to ninety-two, had been Vicar of Bitton before him, so that the soil was worked by Ellacombe hands for more than eighty years.

Canon Ellacombe was scholarly but thoroughly sociable, a good business man and an ardent reformer of his parish. He spent many holidays on the Continent, where he collected plants in a handkerchief tied to an alpenstock, and took with him such holiday reading as the works of Horace and the *Tourist's Flora*. He was an amateur architect and designed a new roof for Bitton church, and he was soaked in the classics—it was his custom to rest on a couch before dinner and compose Latin verses which he read to his family during the meal. He was also an expert on the flowers of Shakespeare and the art of angling.

His garden at Bitton was not large, only one-and-a-half acres, and was not consciously landscaped, but was a home for rare and beautiful plants. The canon totally rejected the horrors of carpet bedding and did not care for studied colour schemes. He grew plants in a mixture, draped his porch with wisteria, smothered the garden walls with Cheddar pinks and other rock plants. There were many plant species, old roses, rare trees and flowering shrubs and plants with beautiful leaves. He liked plants of good form and delighted in dandelions, but abhorred stiff plants like florists' tulips and double zinnias; when given them as presents, he would tell his gardener briskly to throw them away.

The canon exchanged plants with other collectors (he gave Mr Bowles his famous corkscrew hazel) and gave plants away generously, particularly in the village. He believed that most villagers were natural gardeners but lacked plant education and that the garden was the best possible place for a parson to make friends with his parishioners, who might in time be tempted into the house to delve into the books. His botanical and horticultural library was extensive and consulted almost every day.

Of course few parsonage gardens have been blessed with a rector or vicar as gifted as Canon Ellacombe, but there were many in the Victorian age with varied, knowledgeable planting in a homely and serene design.

12

THE COTTAGE GARDEN

HOLLYHOCKS, lavender and roses round the door—most of us carry a cherished picture of the English cottage garden in the mind's eye. But the cottage garden is something much more than a sentimental memory. It has been in its time a bastion of tradition, a sanctuary for plants trembling on the verge of extinction, and an inspiration for gardens larger and finer than itself.

The cottage garden probably came into being after the Black Death, when so many peasants died in the plague that there was land to spare and instead of working strips in the open field for the local lord, a man could amass a little personal plot near his house. This would be stuffed with vegetables but there would also be herbs brought in from the wild— herbs for cooking, medicine, strewing and bunching to take away smells and to discourage fleas. But herbs can be very decorative, and since uneducated people are not insensate it seems highly likely that the cottager would enjoy his flowers and group them carefully. The herbs would all be hardy, and hardy plants have been the core of the cottage flower garden from the Middle Ages through all the centuries until today.

The design of the cottage garden has also been stable. Village people are conservative by nature and for centuries had no space, money or inclination to change one of the simplest and most beautiful shapes of the countryside. A path from the lane to the cottage door, edged with herbs, with vegetables behind the herbs, and one or two fruit-trees and some beehives must have been the basic pattern from the beginning. How far the cottager picked up high-class notions as his prosperity increased is guesswork, but it is tempting to imagine an arbour or rustic arch in a mediaeval cottage garden, a knot or piece of topiary in an Elizabethan garden, and 'improved' and double flowers from the same period. A

number of foreign flowers such as hollyhocks, madonna lilies, tulips, sun-flowers and dahlias certainly found their way into cottage gardens as and when they spread through Britain.

'Cottager' is, of course, a word with many meanings. The early cottagers were poor, and though later they grew more prosperous, theirs is not a long, happy story of increasing wealth and comfort. 'Cottage industry', now a term of approbation, once bred conditions as sweated as anything in the coal-mines. There have been good times and bad times for cottagers, varying with legislation, employment, the weather, and so on. Flora Thompson, in *Lark Rise to Candleford*, tells of the pitiful poverty of her hamlet as late as the 1880s, though the old people in Lark Rise remembered better days and well-stocked gardens, with plenty of flowers and fruit-trees, poultry and bees, before the 19th-century enclosures. In the 18th century, if not earlier, a new bird entered village life to confuse the picture, the genteel cottager. By Jane Austen's time there were plenty of minor gentry, on social terms with the squire and the parson, living in cottages and gardening with the same amateur skill and delight they brought to music, sketching and literature.

In a book of this scope, one has to cut a cross-section, and we have chosen as the epitome a cottage garden in its Victorian heyday. The house, like most old English cottages, even those which claim to be Tudor, is 17th-century, though the garden may be older. The cottager might be an agricultural worker, a retired tradesman, the village shopkeeper, or a village craftsman. In the 18th century, a fair-sized village would have its own saddler, miller, shoemaker, carpenter, wheelwright, mason, black-smith and so on, but in the mid-19th century, perhaps only the blacksmith and the carpenter would be left, and the village shopkeeper would be selling a range of factory-made goods. Any of these might be skilled gardeners, and if the cottager was comfortably off—was thrifty, had married money, or was not too fecund—the garden would be well stocked. There would be a good supply of vegetables, manured with dung and nightsoil, flowers grown usually in rows, but also in mixtures, apple-trees, cherries, gooseberry bushes and other favourite fruits, perhaps an arbour, a bit of topiary, a rustic arch and a seat—a wooden or turf seat near the cottage door, arched with sweet-briar, was a common feature. In the back yard there would be pigs and poultry, a water-butt and a muck-heap.

Tracking down the authentic cottage flowers, as opposed to those which are vaguely called 'old-fashioned', is by no means easy. Sometimes a Constable painting, a village poet like John Clare, a country essayist like Miss Mitford or a garden antiquarian like Mrs Ewing provides a genuine clue. John Clare, in a poem written soon after 1820, tells of a Northamptonshire cottager whose best-loved books were the Bible, the prayer-book, *Pilgrim's Progress* and 'prime old Tusser', presumably Thomas Tusser of the *Hundred Good Points of Husbandry*, so Tusser's plants and plant mixtures, such as strawberries with roses, had stayed the course as cottage favourites for more than two hundred years.

Among the certainties are climbing plants, especially roses, honeysuckle, the everlasting pea or, more rarely, a vine, trained to cottage walls and curling over the porch. As a hedging plant, hawthorn had been the most popular for hundreds of years and remained so, though holly and privet were also common.

Other plants which undoubtedly have a long cottage history are hollyhocks, pinks in great variety, carnations, sweet williams, marguerites, marigolds, madonna lilies, peonies, tulips, crocuses, daisies, foxgloves, violets and pansies, monkshood, lavender, campanulas, mignonette, Solomon's seal, evening primrose, stocks, lily-of-the-valley, single and double primroses and cowslips and many roses from the single sweet-briar to luscious centifolias. Many of these plants would have been brought in from woods and fields, and chance or skill would have improved them. Some cottagers, women as well as men, were florists and grew pinks, tulips or auriculas of exceptional quality. A good cottage garden, unlike a garden stocked with bedding plants, had something in flower all the year round.

To this sort of garden we owe an enormous debt. Loved and cared for over a long period, the cottage garden was never affected by plant-destroying fashions like the parterre, the landscape and the bedding craze, and in its narrow flower-beds, or tucked under hedges and in odd corners, old-fashioned plants survived which would otherwise have been lost forever. Not even the parsonage garden was such a haven for the old plants, for not every parson was a Canon Ellacombe, and many adopted carpet bedding.

There is no doubt at all that many old plants survived in cottage gardens only, outstanding among them rare primroses and pinks. Mrs Ewing's *Mary's Meadow* (1883–4) is a children's story revolving round the rescue from a cottage garden of an old hose-in-hose cowslip. In *Letters from a Little Garden* (1885) she tells us that in the preceding decades gardeners at the big houses had flung herbaceous plants in dozens on to rubbish heaps to make way for bedding plants and that the old flowers could be found in cottage gardens alone. (It is painful to learn from her that Chippendale chairs had likewise gone out of fashion and been chopped up for firewood.) She writes:

> It is such little gardens which have kept for us the Blue Primroses, the highly fragrant summer roses (including Rose de Meaux and the red and copper Brier), countless beautiful varieties of Daffy-down-dillies, and all the host of sweet, various and hardy flowers which are now returning ... from the village to the hall.
>
> It is still in cottage gardens chiefly that the Crown Imperial hangs its royal head. One may buy sheaves of it in the Taunton market-place on early summer Saturdays. What a stately flower it is! and, in the paler variety, of what an exquisite yellow!

The 'stately Crown Imperial' is a quotation from John Parkinson's *Paradisus*, and Mrs Ewing founded a Parkinson Society 'to search out and cultivate old flowers which have become scarce'.

Other lost plants restored to us from cottage gardens are the charming little Fairy Rose (re-introduced by Miss Jekyll), the Rose du Barri primrose, a double cream polyanthus found in Sussex, a scarlet double sweet william found in Ireland (a good hunting-ground), and many old-fashioned pinks, carnations and violas.

In the last quarter of the 19th century, the cottage garden took on a new role, this time a star part. Sickened by the excesses of carpet bedding in the larger gardens, a new generation of gardeners, headed by William Robinson, with supporters like Miss Jekyll, Mrs Ewing and many keen botanists and collectors, turned for inspiration to the cottage garden, and a cottage style, more varied and more sophisticated than the genuine article, has been the reigning fashion ever since.

Robinson's *The English Flower Garden* (1883) was a great piece of polemic writing and perhaps the most influential gardening book ever published in England. Of course, Robinson did not destroy the High Victorian garden at one blow. A reaction to its rigidity was already in the air and the time was ripe for a major attack. Robinson himself was not against formal gardening as such, but thought it should be confined to the space round the house. Beyond the house the ideal should be natural, and plants should never be tortured into uneasy postures. He thundered against standard roses, scrollwork, carpet bedding, statuary, sham Italian gardens, waterworks, and indeed everything Joseph Paxton had stood for. He praised cottage gardens, creepers and ramblers on the house, roses well grouped and underplanted, the loose planting of shrubs, a year-long succession of hardy shrubs, herbaceous plants and bulbs, climbers rambling up fruit-trees, plant species, an orchard wild garden, woodland plants in the garden, and winter flowers. Not all of these are cottage ideas, but the feeling for permanent planting and for plants in happy mixtures is of cottage inspiration.

Robinson, with his books and his magazine, *The Garden*, led the way to this generous kind of planting, and the gardens he inspired were a success at every level.

One of the prototypes was that of his friend and colleague, Miss Gertrude Jekyll, at Munstead Wood, which will be discussed later. Two much larger gardens which still thrive today were made at Hidcote, in the early years of this century, and at Sissinghurst, begun in 1930. Hidcote consists of a series of formal enclosures, each with a different informal planting theme, and Vita Sackville-West, who created Sissinghurst, described Hidcote as 'a cottage garden on the most glorified scale ... there is a kind of haphazard luxuriance, which of course comes neither by hap nor hazard at all'.

Sissinghurst was designed on the same principles. Formal enclosures, linked by arches or straight alleys, are planted with bursts of vegetation.

Old-fashioned flowers abound, there is a herb garden, a sweet-briar hedge, climbing roses, clematis and honeysuckles, an abundance of woodland plants, and something in flower all the year round. Miss Mitford's cottagers would be amused to hear that Hidcote or Sissinghurst was a descendant of their simple gardens, but the link is firm.

From Robinson's time on, more and more gardens were made, and are still being made, with cottage ideals in mind. Perhaps this is more true today than ever, when we use our gardens hard, labour in them ourselves, grow vegetables as though hunger were knocking at the door, and have a primitive longing to be self-sufficient.

13

THE LONDON SQUARE

THE COMMUNAL GARDEN of a residential square is a London speciality with no counterpart abroad. No group has ever understood comfort so well as the English middle class—certainly not the French, with their spindly furniture, nor the Americans, with their hazardous gadgets—and the London square, essentially an upper-middle-class perquisite, is one of the most comfortable garden ideas since the arbour with a turf seat.

There were rough, untended squares in London as far back as the 17th century and improvements were suggested as early as 1722 by Thomas Fairchild, author of *The City Gardener*, who wanted to see the dull grass platts and gravel walks of St James's Square, Lincoln's Inn Fields and other open spaces replaced by wildernesses with birds and a variety of trees. But we owe the well-planned residential square as we know it to the developers of the 19th century. Some of the greatest gardeners had a hand in the early models. Humphry Repton was consulted when the 4th Duke of Bedford was developing Bloomsbury and designed Russell Square, a space of six acres, as well as Bloomsbury Square and Cadogan Square (now Cadogan Place) for other landlords. Needless to say, John Loudon was another who had views on the designing and planting of squares, and he published some useful criticisms.

The Belgravia squares, separated by roads, like other squares, from the large stucco houses they served, were begun in 1825 by Thomas Cubitt, developing for the Marquess of Westminster. The Pimlico squares followed soon after, on a marshy site near the river Thames—Eccleston Square was built on the site of an osier bed. At the same period numerous squares were built at Brompton, Kensington and other select villages which were becoming part of London.

The Pleasure Garden

The jewels of London square design are in Notting Hill, on the Ladbroke Estate, where the ground landlord, James Weller Ladbroke, employed as his first surveyor Thomas Allison, who was a landscape gardener as well as an architect. Serious development of the estate began in the 1840s, and with Ladbroke Square itself and fourteen smaller squares and crescents a completely new ideal was introduced, the houses *backing* on to private gardens which led into the communal garden, with no separating road. (In a few cases, the private gardens were omitted.) Here children could safely play and be watched from the windows of the house. Elderly people could sit in peace and privacy a few yards from home. And the householder was relieved of the cares of garden upkeep, for he paid a subscription into a common fund and the garden was run by a residents' committee.

There is no middle-class, middle-aged Londoner who has not some poignant memory of the London squares of his youth—'middle-aged' is the appropriate word, for the arrival of the universal motor-car and the country weekend diminished the social life of the square, which was most active on Saturdays and Sundays. Those who use the squares today are mere part-timers.

Up to, say, 1930, Ladbroke Square was perhaps the most desirable place in London to bring up a middle-class family. Here, small children made pram friendships which were more satisfactory than the friendships of the park, where every game had to be broken up and the prams wheeled their separate ways at tea-time. Here a mother who had sacked or been given notice by her nursery-maid could deposit her children and continue her own life in the house. Here all could enjoy fine trees, reasonably long walks and neat if sooty shrubberies and flower-beds. Children who lived in these squares and went to one of the many good schools nearby were the envy of their fellows, whom they could patronize with invitations to Sunday tea. Though Notting Hill enjoys a concentration of these squares hidden behind their houses, a few were built in other parts of London. A particularly charming one is Spencer Park, south of the Thames in Wandsworth. In the 1870s the 5th Earl Spencer built twenty handsome family houses round a triangle of communal garden. Each

house had its own large back garden with a gate leading into the shared ground which had, and still has, the feeling of a secret garden—few Londoners have even heard of Spencer Park. The original Victorian planting is almost unchanged, a delight to garden scholars though some of today's residents find it a trifle gloomy. There are clumps of bamboos and the lawns are skirted by evergreen trees and shrubs, including Scotch firs, a deodar cedar, variegated laurels, arbutus, *Rhododendron ponticum* and many hollies. Copper beeches and acacias planted a hundred years ago or more are now of magnificent size and there is a splendid liquidambar. However, one feature has gone, for there was originally a lake.

Much thought was given to the design of squares from the beginning. Repton tried, if the site gave a chance, to provide an undulation. He surrounded his squares with a solid hedge of hornbeam and privet, and inside put a broad gravel walk and then a lawn where children could play. In the centre were lime-trees, annually trimmed, flowers and shrubberies, and in Russell Square there was the added attraction of a bronze statue of the Duke of Bedford.

Loudon's view was that the squares he saw when he first came to London in 1803 were gloomy places with too many lowering yews and pines and other conifers, and he pressed for more deciduous trees, especially planes and sycamores. He thought that every square should have a perimeter walk inside the railings, to get the maximum length, rounded off at the corners, and that there should be one sunny walk, one shady walk, seats and a shelter from sudden rain.

As London grew sootier and foggier, thought had to be given to the choice of plants. It was clear by the middle of the 19th century that conifers could barely survive London grime and that deciduous trees like planes, elms and ailanthus were more suitable, with the plane, renewing its bark as well as its leaves, the best London tree of all. Certain evergreen shrubs could endure the dirt, which is why London was saddled for so long with spotted aucubas, but deciduous shrubs and small trees like lilac, almond and 'Golden Chain' laburnum were more satisfactory. Most squares have an iris walk, for the iris has always been a good Londoner, and most have a few circular beds for bedding plants, with bulbs in the spring and geraniums or *Salvia splendens*, edged with lobelias, to follow.

Now, with jet planes roaring overhead on their homing path to Heathrow, and with the car at the ready to whisk the family away for weekends, the London square has become little more than a dog-walk, where owners with trousers pulled over pyjamas or with a tweed coat thrown over a nightdress lead their dogs for five minutes before breakfast and make another sortie under the stars at night. Sometimes a tennis court provides a sporting amenity. There is still pleasure to be derived from the trees, which, planted a hundred years ago or more, have now reached their full splendour. But the square as a social centre is past its prime.

14

GARDENS EN ROUTE

C ERTAIN GARDENS are rightly designed to produce a quick shock rather than a lingering enjoyment. The railway station, the riverside lock, the municipal promenade, are places where the visitor is on the move and is not going to establish a personal relationship with the gardener and where, therefore, the requirements are a dramatic splash of colour and a technical *tour de force*. No style is better for the purpose than carpet bedding.

Such gardens were in their prime in the late Victorian and the Edwardian years. Then the Thames-side resorts, such as Marlow, Shiplake, Pangbourne, Henley, easily reached by excellent trains, were the goal of delightful excursions from London, and every young man was expected to row or punt. Then a necklace of English seaside resorts from Bognor to Harrogate, from Weston-super-Mare to Weymouth, could count on a select clientèle from July to September. The municipal gardeners were on their mettle.

Gardens to astound the traveller are still very much alive today, nourished by a combination of public finance and private enthusiasm. The municipal carpet displays are, of course, planted by professional gardeners, but the trim formal gardens still to be found at country stations and by rivers and canals are tended as a hobby by the local officials of the authority concerned, who receive either a supply of the plants of their choice or a small cash allowance for raising their own in a greenhouse. Pride is the spur, for visitors never fail to exclaim with wonder at a bright, theatrical display, and there is the further incitement of rivalry with colleagues up the line or down the river. The rail, river and canal authorities run annual competitions for the best garden of the summer, though British Rail, whose station competitions were once a national event, now runs

them in Scotland only. Even so, there are many elderly stationmasters in England who carry on the old tradition with reduced resources— instead of 50 yards of bedding on either platform, tended by a station staff of four or five men, a single survivor keeps a dozen tubs painted shiny white and brimming with geraniums, alyssum and lobelias. His reward is compliments from the passengers as they hand in their tickets.

The original Victorian bedding schemes are today admitted by even the most hide-bound Superintendent of Parks to have been crude in colour, for often only the three primary colours, red, blue and yellow, were used, with no half-colours to soften the harsh stripes of geraniums, lobelias and calceolarias. By the 1880s softer colours and foliage plants had been introduced, and much thought was given to breaking up the plant mass with variety of height.

Every bedding scheme is made with three components, carpet plants, edging plants and dot plants. The first two form the carpet groundwork and are dwarf in size, while the dot plants are there for contrast of height and colour and may include standards as much as 30 inches tall. A typical simple bedding scheme would be an edging of dark blue lobelias, a carpet of begonias and heliotrope, and standard fuchsias for dot plants. Another might be an edging of echeveria, a carpet of verbena and lobelias, and cannas and abutilon for dot plants. Elaborate schemes would require many more varieties and a wide range of foliage plants, like coleus and variegated-leaved geraniums. Some of the most successful bedding plants are rarely used in other contexts and the general gardener would be hard put to identify the varieties of, say, alternanthera, mesembryanthemum or ageratum.

Most bedding displays are of geometric pattern, though sometimes a borough emblem, a floral clock or a motto gives nostalgic pleasure, often planted on a tilted bank so that the passer-by in train, boat or motor-car can get the message at a glance. Fortunately, our borough councils have to date eschewed political slogans, unlike some authorities behind the Iron Curtain. The hammer and sickle picked out in geraniums or the motto 'religion is the opium of the people' in heliotrope has not yet appeared in our municipal planting schemes. The floral emblems and sentiments chosen have been acceptable to all.

Even the doughtiest champions of the natural garden, such as William Robinson, Mrs Ewing or Miss Jekyll, admitted that bedding is sometimes justified, and the riverside garden, with its brief summer season and its passing crowd, is just the right place.

15

THE SURREY SCHOOL

IN 1889 a formidable, sharp-tongued, middle-aged lady who was a painter, a blue-stocking, a wit and a celebrated gardener met a charming young architect at a tea-party. She lived in Surrey and the young man, whose parents had a house at Thursley, was just beginning to alter and design houses in the same county. They were Miss Gertrude Jekyll and Edwin Landseer Lutyens.

The meeting was a historic occasion, for these two were to become friends and collaborators for life and to introduce a new kind of gardening in what is known as the Surrey style. William Robinson, a close friend and journalistic colleague of Miss Jekyll since 1875, is usually recognized as the leader of the Surrey school. But Robinson was the champion of the 'natural' garden from which Miss Jekyll was, perhaps unconsciously, moving away, and it is the Lutyens–Jekyll partnership which is the core of Surrey gardening—a harmony of informal planting within a formal structure.

Miss Jekyll and Lutyens had much in common. Both came from large happy families. Both had a physical handicap, for Miss Jekyll had defective eyesight and Lutyens was a delicate child who had to be educated at home. Both had been art students. Both loved Surrey above all other counties, she having studied its flora from childhood and liking its acid sandy soil, he attracted by its picturesque tradition of building. Both had a passion for craftsmanship. Miss Jekyll had been strongly influenced by Ruskin, William Morris and the arts and crafts movement and there was almost no craft which she did not practise with her own large but skilful hands—carving, gilding, metal-work, embroidery and, of course, gardening, for which she wore heavy boots which were immortalized in a painting by William Nicholson. She loved hand tools, even axes and mat-

tocks, and when she took up photography, she did her own processing. She enjoyed even the noises of craftsmanship when good men were at work. Few would share her enthusiasm for 'the ringing music of the soft-tempered blade cutting a well-burnt brick', 'the small melodious scream of the well-sharpened plane as it shoots along the edge of the board and gives out its long, fragrant ribbon of shaving', or 'the beating of the cow-hair that is mixed with the wall plaster', but it was all an essential part of her love for everything handmade.

Lutyens, too, was an admirer of William Morris and had a great feeling for traditional materials, for local stones and antique finishes, and in his early houses he used half-timbering. The two were born to be partners and they met at a critical moment when Miss Jekyll's eyesight was failing; she knew that she would not be able to paint much longer and she was looking for a new outlet for her creative energy. She had already designed a number of gardens for friends and clients, but it had been a secondary interest to fine art.

Lutyens and Miss Jekyll decided almost at once to collaborate and, in the words of her nephew, Francis Jekyll, 'to fill the countryside with homes and gardens, frames and canvases for living and changing pictures, where the infinite possibilities of hill and valley, of wall, water and woodland might be exploited to the full'. They set to work in 1891 and commissions came quickly. In 1896, Lutyens built a new house for Miss Jekyll herself in a clearing in a wood at Munstead, near Godalming, a stone's throw from the house where she had been living with her widowed mother, who died in 1895. This house was to be small but perfectly proportioned, with every detail down to the door handles and window catches craftsman made—and it was to have 'a little of the feeling of a convent'.

The house Lutyens built, called Munstead Wood, was an honest building of local stone and local oak and had many of the Lutyens features which were later to be writ larger in country houses all over England. It was gabled and had tall chimneys and low casement windows. Inside, there were a big stone fireplace, a long gallery and beams of seasoned oak and outside there were half-timbering, an oak-framed porch, a small paved court leading down to a sunk rectangular pool and plenty of stone

98

steps leading up, down and everyway. There were also high garden walls of local sandstone.

Miss Jekyll's property was of 15 acres, including the woodland, a mature plantation of oaks, silver birches and nut-trees with an occasional pine, and here, even before the house was built, she began to make a garden in the style which was her own. It was a painter's garden, a garden of conscious pictures, with every corner or glade thoughtfully composed. She was as much a pictorial gardener in her way as William Kent.

The house itself she softened with climbers like clematis and vine and with rosemary at the foot of the walls. She had always loved the aromatic sub-shrubs of the Mediterranean, like rosemary, lavender, phlomis and cistus, since a happy journey to Greece and Turkey in her youth. The court near the house she treated formally, with pots of lilies and cannas and balls of clipped box. Ferns fringed the pool.

Steps descended from the court to a lawn, and paths led from the lawn into the woodland and to all the picturesque places in the garden, of which there would always be at least one in its glorious prime. For each section of the garden was devoted to a season, so that all the plants there would reach their peak together, and when their day was finished, their climax over, another part of the garden would begin to bloom. This seasonal planting was one of Miss Jekyll's fundamental principles.

One of the earliest and loveliest garden pictures of the year was in the woodland where, among the nut-trees and birches, Miss Jekyll planted a carpet 100 yards long of polyanthus of her own selected strain, all yellow and white but varied in their detail. Another woodland picture followed soon after, in May, when scented azaleas flowered among the silver birches, with tongues of ferns, bergenias, hellebores, heathers and small shrubs running in among them.

From July to October the most spectacular feature of the whole garden was in flower—a wide border nearly 200 feet long backed by an 11-foot wall, with large drifts of flowers in carefully planned colour schemes. At each end of the border the flowers were blue, white and pale yellow with grey foliage plants. These melted into groups of purple, white and pink flowers with more grey foliage plants, and the two met in the middle in a blaze of orange and red. Bold groups of yuccas marked the extremities of the border and the corners where the border was broken by a path and gateway. With the herbaceous plants were mingled hydrangeas, dahlias, pelargoniums, cannas, half-hardy annuals like salpiglossis and tobacco plant, and some roses. There were other borders in the garden in special colour schemes—one was entirely purple, white and grey—and there were special gardens for special flowers, notably a peony garden and a Michaelmas daisy garden. There were many flowery incidents throughout both garden and wood—a patch of trillium and Solomon's seal or of fox-glove and bracken, or a planting of azaleas with cistuses. There was a winter picture of heathers, hellebores and glossy-leaved bergenias; there was a long sunny bank of briar roses; there was a rock garden and a pergola garden and a kitchen garden with vegetable beds bordered with flowers.

As the garden grew, and its fame spread all over the world, it became a place of pilgrimage for visitors. The great gardeners came, of course, like William Robinson, Miss Ellen Willmott and (in 1909) the Countess von Arnim, or 'Elizabeth of the German garden', but so many strangers applied for permission to visit Munstead Wood that they became something of a burden. Some were mere rubberneckers and asked stupid questions, and as Miss Jekyll never suffered fools gladly, they probably got tart answers. But as she had taken to writing successful books on gardening (the first, *Wood and Garden*, came out in 1899), and also to selling surplus plants, she could hardly hope for complete privacy. She was also an early contributor to the new magazine, *Country Life*, which was to be the showcase in future years of Lutyens houses and Jekyll gardens.

Since Miss Jekyll had been gardening and studying plants long before she met Lutyens, perhaps her ideas should be set out before one considers how far she had to modify them in working with the collaborator who was to outstrip her in fame. (*The Dictionary of National Biography*, always thin on gardeners, gives her no place.)

Miss Jekyll believed in a garden as a series of pictures, so she insisted on careful planning. Never buy plants, she said, and then look for a spot to place them but plan your spaces and then buy. She made scale plans on paper of every bed before it was planted, with the colour scheme and number of plants required exactly worked out.

Her great speciality was the herbaceous border, which she planted always with flowers in horizontal drifts, never in blocks. The hot colours in the border were always in 'graduated harmonies, culminating into gorgeousness' but the cool colours like blue needed some contrasts of white or pale yellow. She planted in masses, avoiding too many varieties for a given space, so that the borders were never bitty. She deplored bittiness in the lawn as much as in the border and thought it ruined the serenity of a garden. Why spoil a peaceful stretch of lawn by dotting it with specimen trees? She wanted 'to keep down the shop-window feeling, and the idea of a worthless library made up of single odd volumes where there should be complete sets'. (There was a totally opposite and equally valid school of thought contemporary with Miss Jekyll led by that greatest of plantsmen, E. A. Bowles. Mr Bowles objected to 'the school of gardening that encourages the selection of plants merely as artistic furniture, chosen for colour only, like ribbons or embroidery silk'. Each plant was an individual in his eyes.)

Miss Jekyll thought the gardener should cultivate a good eye for flowers, should be intolerant of rubbish and should discard bad plants and not be tempted by sheer size. She used foliage plants beautifully, especially bergenias, hostas, silver plants and grasses. She appreciated plants of quality whether they were foreigners or natives. Big, sharp plants like yuccas were important to her, but so were many cottage flowers, and she rediscovered old-fashioned flowers which had been nearly lost during the bedding craze—one of her favourite old cottage plants was the delicate little Fairy Rose. Every plant must be good of its kind and, indeed, she improved many flowers herself by selection, such as the Munstead primroses.

One of her special skills was melting the hard into the soft. Where a lawn joined a wood there would be a soft fringe of shrubs to avoid a jolt between the two—perhaps rhododendrons, perhaps hollies with rambler roses scrambling into them. Steps and walls were softened with tufts of plants; dry walls would sprout ferns and rock plants and high walls might have a rambler rose, like her favourite 'The Garland', tumbling over from above. This gift was a godsend when she worked with Lutyens, who was prodigal in his use of stone.

She liked pergolas, which were much in fashion at the turn of the century. Usually she grew vines, jasmine, clematis or wisteria over them rather than roses. She loved scented flowers, from the dry, aromatic herbs of the Mediterranean to the wild violets of the English woods, and wished she had space for a garden of wallflowers. She delighted in wild gardening but said that of all forms of gardening, it is the most difficult.

Such was Miss Jekyll's philosophy of gardening expressed in her articles and books, and it dovetails exactly with the creed of William Robinson.

But did it work out like this in practice? In her early gardens it probably did, and certainly her own garden at Munstead Wood was a perfect expression of her ideas. It must have been picturesque and serene. But when Lutyens got into his stride, the vision of a natural garden was lost in a new, hard framework. Lutyens was an architect who carried his building from the house far out into the garden and his gardens are both formal and extremely complicated. Terraces, steps, pools, pillars, pergolas, niches, in stone or brick or tiles or all three together, make a Lutyens garden an architectural *tour de force* rather than a home from home for plants. The triumph of his gardens is his use of materials. Using local materials always—yellow rubblestone in Surrey or Yeovil ashlar in Somerset—he achieved miracles of architectural detail. Overhanging treads created light and shade on a flight of steps. Specially made thin bricks gave grace to a pergola. Inlay of one material in another, such as brick or lead in stone, gave rich texture to a paved terrace. The rectangular lines of a garden were broken by semi-circular sweeps of steps or by looped ribbons of stone in a straight paved walk. Miss Jekyll's task was no longer to paint garden pictures, but to soften the hardness of these brilliant *jeux d'esprit*. She believed increasingly in the interdependence of gardening and architecture, perhaps even yielding the palm to architecture, for in the early 1900s, when she was barely sixty, she ceased to visit the gardens where she was working unless they were near Munstead, but contributed paper plans from home. This was surely an abdication of responsibility.

However, she did her task of softening the new gardens wonderfully well. She planned for new walls to be masked with roses or banks of rosemary, for flowers to be sown or planted in the interstices of bricks or stone. Formal ponds were planted informally with reeds and marsh plants, formal rose-beds edged with thick frills of bergenias, and she made lavish use of ground-cover plants like pinks, hostas, bergenias and *Stachys lanata* to spill over from a flower-bed on to the path. In every garden there was at least one noble herbaceous border where she could use her favourite colours and plants, simple lavender, catmint, grasses and wild soapwort rubbing noses with the most glorious lilies, tall verbascums, handsome campanulas, China roses and perhaps a few small shrubs like *Iberis sempervirens* or *Rhododendron ferrugineum*.

Although most of the Lutyens–Jekyll gardens were made as late as the present century, their charm has already passed away. Many exist with the architecture in good shape and the planting plans safe in some library, but the enormous resources needed to keep up such a garden today are non-existent. Lutyens was as careless of convenience or economy outside the house as he was inside, and his little mosaic pieces of lawn, requiring two men to lift a lawn-mower up or down his multitudinous steps, are hopelessly unpractical. A Lutyens garden in its prime needed up to twenty gardeners to manage it. Nor was Miss Jekyll ahead of her time in the matter of saving labour. In her own garden at Munstead, the woodland primroses (all hundred yards of them) were taken up, divided and replanted every year by herself, with three men and a boy, and the herbaceous border was refurbished several times in a season. So most of the Surrey School gardens are mere ghosts today.

However, one wonderful restoration was undertaken at Hestercombe House, near Taunton, in 1973, which every student of the Edwardian garden should see. Hestercombe is a large Victorian house (untouched by Lutyens) with a Lutyens–Jekyll garden begun in 1904. It is now the headquarters of the Somerset Fire Brigade and, when some of the Jekyll planting plans were found in a shed in 1970, the enterprising Chief Fire

Officer got in touch with the County Architect, and to the credit of all the authorities concerned, restoration was agreed. Each year a new piece of the garden is taken in; crumbling architecture is repaired and the beds sensitively and correctly planted.

The garden, which is perhaps Queen Anne in feeling, is built round a large central sunk plat with formal flower-beds. It shows nearly every facet of Lutyens's garden talent. There are a pergola walk, a Dutch garden, formal rills of water, elaborate pools, and everywhere fine and varied brick and stone work—on one terrace, old mill-wheels have been sunk into the paving. There is also a complete Lutyens building, a beautiful orangery made of a combination of dressed yellow Ham stone from the Yeovil district and undressed pink stone quarried from the combe behind the house. Miss Jekyll did not visit Hestercombe herself but designed all the planting from home, including a fine grey herbaceous border near the house and exquisite marsh plants beside the narrow rills.

Miss Jekyll continued to work with Lutyens over many years, though when public building took up an increasing proportion of his time, she worked sometimes with other architects and sometimes on her own. The two remained friends always, and when in her late eighties her indomitable energy flagged, he gave her an invalid chair for travelling round her garden. After her death he wrote a charming reminiscence of their friendship, saying that she had the courage and bearing of a true *grande dame*.

When she was at the peak of her career before the first World War, Miss Jekyll's reputation began to extend beyond this country to the Continent and, more markedly, to the United States, and she was asked to design gardens for French, Belgian and American connoisseurs. Though she gladly advised the discriminating Americans who wrote to her, she appreciated that the American climate is hostile to English planting; her ideas on simplicity, mass planting and perhaps the conception of a cultivated glade could be exported across the Atlantic, but not much more.

At home, her influence was overwhelming and as a colourist she is still the model to whom many flower gardeners turn. When she died in 1932 at the age of eighty-nine, she had designed wholly or partly more than two hundred gardens in her full and successful life.

A final postscript has not much to do with gardening, but gives an insight into the originality of Miss Jekyll's character. She said that people could be divided into two classes, armigerous and non-armigerous, each with expressions of their own. For instance, armigerous people say *great-coat*, not *overcoat*; they *have* tea, they don't *take* tea; they say *waistcoat*, not *vest*; they never go to the dress circle of a theatre, but only to the stalls; they never use an eggcup to hold up the pastry in a pie. She made these distinctions half seriously, half with tongue in cheek—some thirty years before Nancy Mitford entertained us with U and non-U.

16

THE JAPANESE GARDEN

THE JAPANESE VOGUE has no great significance in the broad stream of English garden history. It was a charming, rather dotty aberration confined to approximately thirty years between about 1880 and 1910, but there was a sound reason for it.

Until the middle of the 19th century, Japan was one of the most impenetrable countries in the world. Even China, having well-worn trade routes to the west, was not enclosed in such a thick cocoon. Soon after 1850, with internal political change followed by external treaties with the United States and Europe, the mystery package burst open, and in the last quarter of the century the artistic treasures of Japan became the joy of the western connoisseur. There were lacquered screens and knick-knacks in the English drawing-room, Japanese prints on the walls, kimonos and fans in the wardrobe, geisha girls teetering and tinkling on the stage. In 1885, Gilbert and Sullivan parodied the Japanese mania in *The Mikado* and in 1904 Puccini treated it tragically in *Madam Butterfly*. Among the Japanese arts to root sporadically in Britain was that of gardening.

There are three distinct kinds of Japanese garden, the water garden, the dry garden (which includes the Zen-Buddhist contemplative gardens of stone and sand), and the tea garden, but we are concerned with only one kind here. It was the Japanese water garden which the British took to their hearts. True, they usually got it all wrong, for, except for a few who had travelled to Japan, the English gardener did not attempt to understand Japanese gardening, and what he usually achieved was a dinky picture with an oriental bridge. But the Japanese idea of gardening, based on symbolism, is so alien to our own that a vague impression was probably just as sensible as a carbon copy.

The Japanese garden is essentially an imitation landscape. It may be

106

as small as a tea-tray or be measurable in acres, but everything in it must be exquisitely placed and of perfect proportion. A garden a few feet square will suggest, with mossy stones, shingle, dwarfed pines, tiny clipped shrubs, tufts of grass and ferns, a rocky seascape or the grand panorama Fujiyama. A larger garden may have a lake, bridges, ledges of rock, trees and shrubs, islands, stepping stones, imitation jungles and rice-fields, bronze cranes, stone lanterns, pagodas and pavilions, but all must be in scale, with trees pruned and shrubs clipped to the necessary size. Such a garden is the height of artifice, a landscape seen through a diminishing glass. Flowers are few and not important. The Japanese garden is neither colourful nor highly scented. Groups of irises will rise from the water and the clipped, rounded bushes of azaleas and camellias will flower in their season, but that is a secondary consideration to their form. Flowers for flower arranging are grown in separate beds away from the pleasure garden.

Reginald Farrer, botanist, traveller, rock gardener and writer, lived for a year in Japan in 1903, learned the language, had a house and garden of his own, and visited and appreciated gardens and nurseries all over the islands. He concluded that the Japanese were not flower lovers but tor-turers of plants who 'brutalized' and 'harried' them to achieve a perfect composition or symbolic effect. Moreover, the Japanese accept (or accepted in Farrer's day) only eleven plants as being fully worthy:

A flower [he wrote in his book *The Garden of Asia*] to be admitted by Japanese canons, must conform to certain rigid rules. No flower that fails to do so can be recognized. At the head of rejected blossoms stand the rose and the lily, both of which are considered by the Japanese rather crude, unrefined efforts of nature . . . The elect are cherry, wis-teria, peony, willow-flower, iris, magnolia, azalea, lotus, peach, plum and morning-glory.

There is little affinity between this Japanese perfectionism and the English tradition of catholic plantsmanship.

Nevertheless, a number of Japanese gardens were made in Britain around the turn of the century, when the cult of Japan gripped the western imagination. One which can still be seen in very good order was made on his return from Japan in 1901 by an English diplomatist, the Hon. Louis Greville, at Heale House, in Wiltshire. He not only imported a charming Japanese tea-house of wood and thatch with sliding paper screens, but brought over four Japanese workmen to erect it and to construct a water garden round it. A bridge, a miniature pagoda and stone lanterns are thoughtfully placed, and willow, bamboos, Japanese maples, irises and a rare *Cercidiphyllum japonicum*, a symbol of unified love, are planted in the water meadows. Other famous Japanese gardens were made in the 1890s at Friar Park, Henley, by Sir Frank Crisp, and at Holland House, Kensington, by the 5th Lord Ilchester and his wife, but this was loosely oriental rather than authentic. Contemporary photographs show a medley of exotic plants from all over the globe, with lilies sticking up rather strangely from round holes cut in the lawn.

Other Japanese gardens were made in Scotland and Ireland—one highly elaborate garden was made in Scotland in 1907 by one of those indomitable lady travellers who emerged in the Victorian age. Miss Ella Christie had travelled extensively in Central Asia and the Far East with no regular companion but her maid, even penetrating Tibet. When she reached Japan she fell in love with Japanese gardens and made friends with a similarly obsessed Miss Ella du Cane, who was painting the gardens of Kyoto. On her return to her Perthshire home, Miss Christie brought over 'a little woman, Taki Honda by name, from the Royal School of Garden Design at Nagoya', who laid out and largely constructed herself (heaving and grouping the enormous boulders) a garden in traditional form according to the ancient rule of the Imperial Palace gardens of Japan. It was heavy with symbolism, with a great stone lantern, a Waiting Stone, a Hand-Washing Fountain, a Shinto shrine on the crest of a simulated Fujiyama, stepping stones, lines of willows, Korean pines and a hundred other Japanese features. Later, a Japanese gardener who had lost all his family in an earthquake came to Scotland as Miss Christie's gardener and stayed for many years, a pathetic little brown man who spoke very little English. Matsuo was a Christian and one hopes his religion cheered him up.

Horticulturally speaking, such a garden would be ideally sited, for the whole of Japan is on acid soil, and the peaty soil and high rainfall of much of Scotland, Ireland and the north of England would be hospitable to Japanese plants. Two exceptional Japanese water gardens made at the same period in Ireland at Tully, Co. Kildare, and Powerscourt, Co. Wicklow, are fully maintained today.

Another, quite different Japanese-inspired garden was made in the 1890s by Algernon Freeman-Mitford, later Lord Redesdale, at Batsford Park, Gloucestershire. He went to Japan in 1866 as secretary to the first British Minister appointed under the new *entente*, became deeply involved in Japanese history and culture and was the author of *Tales of Old Japan*. He frankly loathed the Japanese garden as being a doll's-house toy, 'all spick and span, intensely artificial, a miracle of misplaced zeal and wasted labour'. He even had the nerve to make an English garden in Tokyo planted with *Iris kaempferi* in bold masses, which broke his gardener's heart but gave pleasure and amusement to Japanese friends, who found it 'pardonable in a barbarian'. But he was fascinated by Japanese plants, particularly bamboos, and at Batsford Park he made a bamboo garden with some fifty distinct types. Japanese plant nomenclature at this time was in something of a fog, and Freeman-Mitford, working with English botanists and nurserymen, did much to sort out the muddle and to get bamboos introduced and propagated at home.

The Japanese garden in Britain soon went out of fashion, but the interest in Japanese plants came to stay. As soon as Japan opened her doors to the West, collectors began to visit the country looking for new plants, among the earliest being two rivals who both arrived circa 1860, John Gould Veitch and Robert Fortune, who was yet another in the long line of distinguished Scottish collectors. Japanese conifers, primulas, lilies, camellias, tree peonies, bamboos, chrysanthemums, maples and weigelas came here in increasing quantities. Later, in the present century, E. H. Wilson, more famous for his Chinese discoveries, collected cherries and azaleas in Japan, and many Japanese ornamental cherries were brought home, propagated and hybridized by Captain Collingwood Ingram, popularly known as 'Cherry' Ingram, who collected some fifty varieties in cultivation and in the wild, and bred many more in his garden in Kent. Unfortunately, gardeners have not always been discriminating in their choice from so much wealth, and it is dull varieties like 'Kanzan', of awkward shape and with little autumn colour, which line so many suburban streets.

The Japanese style has survived in England in one curious form. Bonsai, or the art of dwarfing trees and shrubs by pruning, is a flourishing hobby, with specialist societies devoted to the subject and books on bonsai on display in every branch of W. H. Smith.

17

THE SUBURBAN GARDEN

THE SUBURBAN GARDEN is the most important garden of the 20th century and there is no excuse other than ignorance for using the word 'suburban' in a derogatory sense. 'It's neither one thing nor the other' is the criticism of people who live in town flats and have a second home in the country, leading two half-lives instead of one whole one. Shoddy planning and jerry-building occur in suburbia as everywhere else, but they are not essential to it, and it is a statistical fact that most family people in Britain would rather have a suburban house than any other kind of home. A suburban house is compact and private, and it allows the owners to create their own world; its garden has advantages to match.

A suburban garden is always compact and usually rectangular. The first planned London suburb, Bedford Park, a late 19th-century development distinguished by houses designed by Norman Shaw, has gardens of wayward shapes, including polygons and wedges, planted with romantic variety by consciously artistic owners. But these are not typical. Today, the rectangle is the norm, a rectangle which becomes smaller with every new development, as the price of land rockets. The suburban garden is neat as well as compact, for with solid boundaries of brick or fencing and with no great weed problem, there is no excuse for losing control. (In a country garden, every wind comes laden with weed seeds.) To enhance the neatness, the house walls are usually kept free of climbing plants, for the suburban housewife does not view earwigs in the bath with favour.

Like the house, the garden enjoys privacy. Sited behind the house, which is probably on a quiet avenue, the suburban gardener can keep himself *to* himself unless there is a rackety brood next door or a neighbour with a power saw. In fact, the garden is ideal for family leisure, and it

is the suburban gardener who is the chief target of those plushy advertisements for garden chairs, pub-style wrought-iron tables, pools and sun umbrellas, swings and climbing frames, sundials and bird-tables and other garden comforts and decorations.

But it is as a creative challenge that the suburban garden has its greatest appeal. Within this rectangle a man (less frequently his wife, for a suburban garden is a man's domain) can attempt to realize the perfect garden of his mind's eye. He can make a rose garden or a rock garden, he can worship his lawn or cultivate flowering shrubs, he can follow a primitive instinct to be self-supporting and make it a miniature small-holding, or he can fulfil his artistic self by making a mosaic of small beds filled with colourful bedding plants.

In spite of this apparent freedom of choice, the suburban garden tends to fall into clichés of both design and planting, for the very good reason that none of us (and this applies to all gardeners, even the greatest) is as original as we like to think. Every gardener is imitative, and as the suburban gardener has only a narrow choice of models to look at, the same ideas and the same plants crop up in every neighbourhood. Five types of suburban garden are particularly popular.

Outstanding is the garden of lawn and roses, the lawn more velvety and the roses more sumptuous than in any other kind of garden. Many suburbs in the Home Counties are built on a rich, slightly acid clay which is ideal for both roses and turf. The upkeep of the lawn often amounts to a religious observance, and members of the cult have been known to cut their lawns in summer one-eighth of an inch every day. The roses are well cultivated, being conscientiously pruned, fed and sprayed, and war is waged and won against mildew, blackspot, greenfly and thrips. The choice of flowers tends to be monotonous, with the same hybrid teas and floribundas appearing in nearly every garden in a street—Super Star, Piccadilly, Fragrant Cloud, Wendy Cussons and Elizabeth of Glamis, Masquerade, Orangeade and Iceberg. The most popular colours are salmon and vermilion. Often there is a climbing or rambler rose, perhaps Danse du Feu or Schoolgirl, trained to fence or pergola, rarely on the house.

A second kind of garden, particularly popular in the suburbs of northern cities, is devoted largely to rock plants, and here the gardener is almost certainly a collector and specialist. A rock garden is rarely beautiful as a piece of landscape (even Kew Gardens has signally failed to make it so, though the Cambridge Botanic Garden has done better) and the interest must lie in the plants. The alpinist may start unambitiously with aubrieta, arabis and a saxifrage or two, but the doll's-house charm and infinite range of available plants will soon ensnare him and he will become a collector. He will buy the best rocks and make subtle soil mixtures and will acquire a greenhouse when he graduates to the high alpines which need dry, pure air.

A newer kind of garden which has come to suburbia since the war is the shrub garden, shrubs being the most important of all post-war plant trends. It is not wholly suited to the suburbs, for shrubs need space, and the suburban shrub and small-tree fancier is driven to timid scaled-down versions of larger plants. The prostrate juniper, the fastigiate cherry, the columnar cypress are dotted about his garden in an almost gardenesque manner. However, various factors, such as the fine shrub displays at flower shows and the new national recreation of visiting famous gardens, have widened the range of shrubs grown and suburban gardens where once forsythia and the common lilac reigned are now enriched with azaleas, camellias, magnolias, brooms, witch hazel, pieris, mahonia, Japanese maples, snakebark maple, winter-sweet and all sorts of curiosities, and the privet or laurel hedge has been replaced by clipped cypress or *Lonicera nitida* (often regretted as the years go by and the cypresses grow too robust and the *Lonicera* goes ragged). Not all the changes are for the better.

Then there is the greenhouse expert, and the addict will spend more money on his greenhouse than he admits to himself, let alone to his wife, adding more gadgets every season and taking rising fuel costs in his stride. He may be a specialist in greenhouse plants such as cacti, orchids or hybrid cyclamen, or he may concentrate on raising plants for bedding out. The number of plants which can be grown in a microscopic greenhouse never fails to amaze the outdoor gardener, as he sees hundreds of exquisitely neat boxes of plants emerging from a mere dog-kennel in early summer.

Lastly, there is the suburban vegetable garden, which has had its ups and downs in this century, rising to a peak in World War II, then declining sharply, but rising again in the 1970s, when the price of shop-bought vegetables made a little effort in the garden well worth while. A greenhouse, a frame with soil-warming cables, or cloches are often used to increase output, and every week the popular gardening magazines will press new gadgets, new soil packs, new tools and new best-ever varieties of seeds upon the receptive husbandman. By far the most prestigious of his crops is the tomato, which has the same sort of cachet as lobster or grouse in more extravagant households.

As a general rule, the suburban garden is the best-kept garden in Britain. The large country garden is defeated by shortage of labour. The agricultural worker's cottage garden is often a slum, for the man who has worked on the land all day loathes gardening in his spare time. The town garden may be delightful but often faces insuperable difficulties such as deep shade, poor soil and marauding cats. The suburban gardener may have limited ambitions, but he usually achieves them.

18

THE PATIO

EVERY YEAR the town garden gets smaller and more precious as developers squeeze us together to make room for luxury offices. To counter the shrinkage the householder calls into use every fraction of space that can house a pot-plant or provide foothold for a garden chair. A roof, a balcony, even a window-box can fulfil the primitive longing to watch things grow, and luckiest of all is the city dweller with a patio.

A patio—the word of course is Spanish—is estate-agent's language for a backyard, and there is something inspiring in the high-sounding name. For while it is all too easy to allow a backyard to become a sordid site for naked dustbins, it is impossible to neglect a patio. Here, in the heart of his home, the owner re-lives the holidays he has spent in southern Europe; here he paves and plants in the Mediterranean manner; here he quaffs *vin rosé* and serves *scampi provençale*. A patio is as much a dream garden as Chatsworth or Sissinghurst and gives far less trouble.

An English patio is not so much a garden as an outdoor room, an inner extension of house or flat which provides instant fresh air on every balmy day. It is a garden for professional people who have no time for manual labour and no intention of allowing the garden to become a drag, and it is a garden for adults, where children must share their elders' pleasures or else make for the nearest playground. They cannot kick a ball about but they can tuck into Sunday lunch out of doors.

Being virtually a room without a ceiling, the patio gives scope for individuality in the choice of floor, walls and furniture. The floor is occasionally cobbled but usually paved, sometimes mistakenly with coloured slabs, and a luxury touch in keeping with the Spanish theme may be a bubble of water in a tiny pool. Walls are more difficult, being usually hideous, grimy and too high, and the choice lies between a coat of paint and some sort of

117

screening. Unfortunately most of the available mass-produced screening is of execrable design, from the daunting wall of pierced concrete down to the interwoven panel fencing which looks as if it were about to collapse and usually is. A simple wood trellis is often the camouflage that works best.

The furniture of the patio is provided by statues and plant containers, bought in junk-shops or garden centres or brought home from sorties to Italy or Spain. Pots, troughs, tubs, and also raised beds and pockets of soil in the paving, are filled with the best readymade compost, for when working on so small a scale, money is no object.

The plants chosen are mostly of Mediterranean origin, such as dwarf cypresses, lavender, bay, kitchen herbs for cooking Elizabeth David recipes, perhaps a *Ficus* of sorts or an arbutus or myrtle. If the patio is heavily shaded, sun-loving plants have to be sacrificed in favour of ivies, hostas, ferns, lilies-of-the-valley, periwinkles and the ever-tolerant box. Most of the plants are bought in a garden centre and failures are quickly thrown out, for the patio is no place for botanical experiment or dying foliage. Sometimes a climber or creeper is grown against one wall to give greenery and height, but by some law of nature it always flowers best over the wall and many a clematis or honeysuckle has reserved its fairest blossoms for the people next door. In spite of this sort of setback, and in spite of the passing Concorde, the neighbours' hi-fi and swarms of troublesome cats, the patio remains one of the most sought-after and best-loved gardens of today. Perhaps its very smallness and its enclosing walls are assets, giving the owner a sense of security.

*   *   *   *   *

This book started with a peristyle and ends with a patio and may seem to be a journey from courtyard to courtyard; but the pattern is fortuitous. In the intervening two thousand years, the garden has expanded and contracted, moved all round the house, been sheltered by walls or thrown open to the country, been a virgin site for the architect or a paradise for the plantsman. To peer into the future of gardening is as foolish as forecasting population trends, where one good plague can upset every calculation.

A single invention, like the deep-freeze, can turn a whole nation into vegetable gardeners, but a total absence of auxiliary labour could switch the exhausted gardener back to paving and trees. The author predicts no inevitable movement in any direction. All that is certain is that future gardens will reflect their time in history and that gardeners will continue to be devoted and adaptable.

BIBLIOGRAPHY
& INDEX

BIBLIOGRAPHY

For a specialist bibliography on garden history, the reader should turn to Miles Hadfield's *A History of British Gardening* (*Gardening in Britain*), which lists several hundred books. My aim here is to select a few books which seem to me to be either exceptionally informative or exceptionally well written and which would lead the amateur historian further along the pleasurable path than I have been able to go in this short survey. I have also included several books published since the last edition of Mr Hadfield's history. Only a few books in my list are in print but all can be consulted in specialist libraries.

Literature is scanty on some aspects of garden history (there is surprisingly little on the cottage garden), but others are so richly documented that any selection is something of a lucky dip. The Landscape Movement has attracted as many writers as has Gothic art and the choice here is embarrassing.

Poetry and fiction are additional sources in which the reader will enjoy finding his own nuggets, sometimes unnoticed by historians. Bound copies of 19th- and 20th-century periodicals are also invaluable, such as *The Gardener's Magazine*, *The Journal of the Royal Horticultural Society*, *The Cottage Gardener*, *The Florist*, *The Garden*, *The Gardener's Chronicle* and *Country Life*.

GENERAL BOOKS

On the history of garden design: J. C. Loudon, *Encyclopaedia of Gardening*; George W. Johnson, *A History of English Gardening*; The Hon. Alicia Amherst (later Cecil), *A History of Gardening in England* (3rd revised edition); Reginald Blomfield, *The Formal Garden in England*; Marie Luise Gothein, *A History of Garden Art*; Inigo Triggs, *Garden Craft in Europe*; H. Avray Tipping, Introduction to *English Gardens* (features from *Country Life*); Miles Hadfield, *A History of British Gardening*; Derek Clifford, *A History of Garden Design*; G. M. Trevelyan, *English Social History*. For biographies of many gardeners, *The Dictionary of National Biography*.

On the history of plants: *The Royal Horticultural Society Dictionary of Gardening* (which includes all dates of plant introductions where known); Canon H. N. Ellacombe, *The Plant Lore and Garden Craft of Shakespeare*; Alice M. Coats, *Flowers*

123

and Their Histories; Roy Genders, *The Cottage Garden*; Wilfrid Blunt, *The Art of Botanical Illustration*.

THE ROMANO-BRITISH GARDEN

R. G. Collingwood and J. N. L. Myres, *The Oxford History of England*, Vol. I; Georgina Masson, *Italian Gardens*; Barry Cunliffe, *Fishbourne: A Roman Palace and its Garden*.

MEDIAEVAL GARDENS

Alexander Neckham, *De Naturis Rerum* and *De Laudibus Divinae Sapientiae* (Rolls Series); Geoffrey Chaucer, *Canterbury Tales* and *The Romance of the Rose*; Canon C. E. Raven, *English Naturalists from Neckham to Ray*; Sir Frank Crisp, *Mediaeval Gardens*; Nicolaus Pevsner, *The Leaves of Southwell*.

THE TUDORS TO THE RESTORATION

William Turner, *A New Herball*; Thomas Tusser, *A Hundred Good Points of Husbandry*; William Harrison, *A Description of England*; John Gerard, *Catalogus Arborum, Fruticum et Plantarum* and *Herball*; William Lawson, *A New Orchard and Garden* and *The Country Housewife's Garden*; Sir Francis Bacon, *On Gardens*; John Parkinson, *Paradisi in Sole Paradisus Terrestris*; John Dent, *The Quest for Nonsuch*; R. T. Gunther, *Early British Botanists and Their Gardens*; Wilfrid Blunt, *Tulipomania*.

FROM 1660 TO 1712

John Evelyn, *Sylva, or a Discourse of Forest Trees*; John Rea, *Flora, Ceres and Pomona*; Sir William Temple, *Upon the Gardens of Epicurus*; Johannes Kip and Leonard Knyff, *Britannia Illustrata*; John Dixon Hunt and Peter Willis, *The Genius of the Place: The English Landscape Garden 1620–1820* (an invaluable anthology); Helen M. Fox, *André Le Nôtre*; David Green, *Gardener to Queen Anne* (a biography of Henry Wise).

THE LANDSCAPE

Joseph Addison, Essays in *The Spectator*; Stephen Switzer, *Ichnographia Rustica*; Alexander Pope, many poems and essays, notably the *Epistle to Lord Burlington*; Sir William Chambers, *A Dissertation on Oriental Gardening*; Gilbert White, *Garden*

Bibliography

Kalendar; Laurence Whistler, *The Imagination of Vanbrugh and His Fellow Artists*; Christopher Hussey, *The Picturesque*; James Lees-Milne, *Earls of Creation*; Dorothy Stroud, *Capability Brown*.

FROM 1800 TO THE 'NATURAL' GARDEN

Humphry Repton, *Observations on the Theory and Practice of Landscape Gardening*; Mary Russell Mitford, *Our Village*; G. W. Johnson, *A History of English Gardening*; William Cobbett, *The English Gardener*; J. C. Loudon, *The Suburban Gardener and Villa Companion* and many other works; Geoffrey Taylor, *The Victorian Flower Garden*; Violet Markham, *Paxton and the Bachelor Duke*; Shirley Hibberd, *Rustic Adornments for Homes of Taste*; A. Tindal Hart, *The Country Priest in English History*.

WILLIAM ROBINSON TO TODAY

William Robinson, *The Wild Garden* and *The English Flower Garden*; Mrs Juliana Ewing, *Mary's Meadow*; Canon H. N. Ellacombe, *In a Gloucestershire Garden*; Gertrude Jekyll, *Wood and Garden, Colour in the Flower Garden* and other books and articles; Reginald Farrer, *The Garden of Asia* and *On the Eaves of the World*; Frank Kingdon Ward, *The Land of the Blue Poppy*; Algernon Freeman-Mitford, *The Bamboo Garden*; The Hon. Alicia Cecil, *English Parks and Gardens*; Francis Jekyll, *Gertrude Jekyll: A Memoir*; Florence Gladstone and Ashley Barker, *Notting Hill in Bygone Days*; J. M. Richards, *The Castles on the Ground*.

INDEX

Addison, Joseph, and landscape movement, 52

Allison, Thomas, gardener-architect, 88

Amherst, the Hon. Alicia (later Cecil), and mediaeval gardens, 16

Anne, Queen, 42, 51, 75, 104; and Hampton Court, 48

Apothecaries' Garden, Chelsea, 60

Arnim, Countess von, 100

Aubrey, John, on London gardening, 46

Austen, Jane, 73, 82; *Mansfield Park*, 59

Bacon, Sir Francis, his dream garden, 29; *On Gardens*, 27

Badminton, 42

Banks, Sir Joseph, in *Endeavour*, 61

Barry, Sir Charles, 72

Batsford Park, Glos., bamboo garden, 110

Bean, W. J., 78

Beaufort, Henry Somerset, 1st Duke of, 42

Beaumont, Guillaume, and Levens Hall gardens, 44–5

Bedford, John Russell, 4th Duke of, Bloomsbury development, 87, 90

Bedford Park, a planned suburb, 112

Blenheim, 51, 58; Great Parterre, 57

Blunt, Wilfrid Scawen, 37

Borra, Giambattista, 55

The Botanical Magazine, 61

Boughton, Montagu estate, 42

Bowles, E. A., 78, 79; objections to Gertrude Jekyll's gardens, 101

Bramham Park, Yorks, French-style park, 42

Bridgeman, Charles, royal gardener, 44; traditional landscape style, 54; and Stowe, 55. 59–60

Brompton Park nursery, Loudon–Wise partnership, 50–1

Brooke, E. Adveno, lithographer, 72

Brown, Lancelot (Capability), and landscape movement, 57–8, 66; his critics, 58–9; and Stowe, 60

Burghley, William Cecil, Lord, 48; Italian-style gardens, 27; and Gerard, 32; foreign purchases, 34

Burlington, Richard Boyle, 3rd Earl of, 52; Italian influence, 55; Pope's 'Epistle' to, 56

Burlington House, 55

Busbecq, Ogier Ghiselin de, in Turkey, 34

Cambridge, Botanic Garden, 115

Castle Howard, 52

Chambers, Sir William, and Kew Pagoda, 57

Charles I, honours Parkinson, 38

Charles II, garden lover, 39; and Hampton Court, 40–1, 47

Chatsworth, 51, 58, 117; classical style layout, 42; Victorian foundation, 67; Great Conservatory, 68

Chaucer, Geoffrey, 15, 20, 22; *Romance of the Rose*, 22

Christ Church, Canterbury, priory garden, 16

Christie, Ella, Japanese garden, 109

Clare, John, 83

Claude Lorraine, landscape paintings, 55, 56

Cobbett, William, the kitchen garden, 67; *The English Gardener*, 16, 67

Country Life, 100

Crisp, Sir Frank, Friar Park garden, 109

Cubitt, Thomas, Belgravia squares, 87

Darwin, Charles, and hybridization, 61

Deptford, Sayes Court garden, 39

Devonshire, William Cavendish, 1st Duke of, and Chatsworth, 42

Devonshire, William Cavendish, 4th Duke of, and Chatsworth, 58

Devonshire, William Caven-